C Self-Study Guide

Jack Purdum

C Self-Study Guide. Copyright © 1985 by Que Corporation.

Library of Congress Catalog No.: LC 84-62752
ISBN 0-88022-149-6

89 88 87 86 85   8 7 6 5 4 3

Interpretation of the printing code: the rightmost double-digit number is the year of the book's printing; the rightmost single-digit number, the number of the book's printing. For example, a printing code of 87-4 shows that the fourth printing of the book occurred in 1987.

Editorial Director
David F. Noble, Ph.D

Editor
Jeannine Freudenberger, M.A.

Book design by
Paul L. Mangin

Cover design by
Listenberger Design Associates

Composed in Megaron
by Que Corporation

Printed and bound by
George Banta Company, Inc.

Dedication

To the cadre of die-hard C programmers and friends of the High Tech Breakfast (HTB) Saturday mornings at Acapulco Joe's.

528298

About the Author

Jack Purdum received a B.A. degree from Muskingum College and M.A. and Ph.D. degrees from Ohio State University. He is currently Associate Professor of Economics at Butler University, where he teaches computer programming and economics courses. Dr. Purdum has received many teaching and research awards, including a National Science Foundation grant to study microcomputers in education. He has published a number of professional articles; a BASIC programming text, and magazine articles in *Byte, Personal Computing*, and *Interface Age*. He is author of *C Programming Guide* and coauthor of *C Programmer's Library*. Dr. Purdum is president of Ecosoft, a software house that specializes in microcomputer software.

Table of Contents

Chapter 1

Chapter 2

Chapter 3

Chapter 4

Chapter 5

Chapter 6

Chapter 7

Chapter 8

Chapter 9

Foreword

This book is a companion self-study volume for the *C Programming Guide* (Purdum, Que Corporation) and is designed to help you start thinking like a C programmer. Because C is different from other languages, various tips and techniques are presented to help you benefit from this powerful language.

The book has nine chapters. Each chapter is divided into two sections. The first section of each chapter contains questions that pertain to specific elements of the C language. My experience in teaching C courses and seminars suggests that certain subjects and concepts are particularly difficult for the beginning C programmer. The questions concentrate on these troublesome areas.

The second section of each chapter presents the answers to the questions posed in the first section. Unlike many texts that give a code fragment to illustrate a topic, this text uses complete, executable programs that you can examine, enter, and run on your computer. Many functions may be worth addition to your standard library of C functions.

I assume two things about the readers of the text. First, you have already read an introductory book on C. Although the topics covered in this book parallel the chapters in the *C Programming Guide*, the material can be used with any book about C. Second, as you read this book, you have access to a computer with a C compiler. There is no substitute for actual programming experience.

As you use this book, you will be tempted to read the question and immediately turn to read the answer. If you do this, you will cheat yourself of the learning experience I am trying to provide. You cannot appreciate the answer if you don't first try to solve the problem for yourself. There is also no reason why you cannot come up with a solution more elegant than the one presented in the book. There is no "single" answer to a programming problem. Reading the answer might thwart your own creative approach to the problem. If you do find a better alternative, I hope you will share it with me. (If you produce something that is truly outstanding, you might even get it published in */c*, Que's C journal!)

For those who don't want to type the programs presented in the text, Que is offering all the programs on disk. An order form is at the end of the book.

There are always a number of people who help bring a book together. Some who helped with this book are Chris DeVoney, Tim Leslie, Alan Stegemoller, Kim Brand, and the staff at Que. I would especially like to thank the many students who suggested the book in the first place; this one's for you.

Jack Purdum, Ph.D.
Tilden Lake, 1984

1
Introduction to C

Questions about the Introduction to C

1.1. What are the fundamental parts from which a C program is built? *(Answer on p. 5.)*

1.2. Why is the `main()` function special? *(Answer on p. 6.)*

1.3. What is a library function? *(Answer on p. 7.)*

1.4. What is an argument? What is an argument list? *(Answer on p. 7.)*

1.5. What is the standard C library? *(Answer on p. 8.)*

1.6. What does it mean when someone says that C is a free-form language? How does this description relate to programming style in C? *(Answer on p. 9.)*

1.7. What types of variables are available in C? *(Answer on p. 10.)*

1.8. Define the data types `char` and `int`. *(Answer on p. 11.)*

1.9. What's wrong with the following program? *(Answer on p. 12.)*

```
#include <stdio.h>
MAIN()
{
    int a, b;
    a = 2;
    b = 3;
    printf("The sum of a and b is %d\n", a + b);
}
```

1.10. What is the general format for using the `printf()` function? *(Answer on p. 12.)*

1.11. What might be done to improve the following program? *(Answer on p. 13.)*

```
#include <stdio.h>

main()
{

    int a, b, c;
    puts("The purpose of this program is to add two");
    puts("numbers together and display the results. ");

    a = 5;
    b = 10;

    c = a + b;

    printf("The sum of %d and %d is %d \n", a, b, c);
}
```

1.12. Your compiler's documentation may have terms you don't know. What do the following terms mean? *(Answer on p. 14.)*

source code
assembler code
assembler
object code
linker
executable code
binary code
librarian

1.13. The %f conversion character is used to print floating-point numbers (table 1.2 in the *Guide*). What does your compiler do with the following program? (This question assumes that your compiler supports floating-point numbers.) *(Answer on p. 16.)*

```
#include <stdio.h>

main()
{

    printf("A floating-point 1 is %f", 1);

}
```

1.14. Letting the tab character be represented by the escape sequence \t and a newline sequence by \n, write a program that uses tabs to draw a box that looks like the following. (The box is tabbed over one position from the left side of the screen.) *(Answer on p. 17.)*

```
+----+
|    |
|    |
+----+
```

Answers to Questions about the Introduction to C

1.1. A C program is written from four elements:

expressions
statements
statement blocks
function blocks

An *expression* is a sequence of variables or constants that are separated by C operators. For example,

```
a = b + c - 2
```

is an expression. In the example, the variables *a* and *b* are separated by the assignment operator, and the variables *b* and *c* are separated by the addition operator. Variable *c* is separated from the constant 2 by the subtraction operator.

A *statement* in C consists of one or more expressions followed by a semicolon (;). Note that

```
a = b + c - 2;
```

is a statement, but the previous example is not because it does not end with a semicolon. A C compiler does not begin processing an expression until the statement terminator (the semicolon) is read.

Obviously, if you forget to end a statement with a semicolon, the compiler will issue an error message. Keep in mind, however, that expressions can be any length. Therefore, the omission of a semicolon at the end of a statement causes the compiler to think that your next statement is part of the first one. As a result, you can get some pretty strange error messages with some compilers because the compiler is lost in the code. You should try leaving out semicolons at the ends of various statements to see how your compiler handles this kind of error and where the compiler "believes" the error has occurred.

A *statement block* consists of one or more statements that are marked by an opening brace ({) and a closing brace (}). A statement block starts with a C keyword (such as for or if) and is usually preceded by an opening parenthesis before the opening brace. For example, a statement beginning with the keyword for might be as follows:

```
for (...) {              /* Dots represent missing */
     statements;         /* details      */
}
```

Note where the opening brace is located in a statement block: after and on the same line with the parentheses. The closing brace should line up under the first letter of the C keyword. Placing braces in this fashion is based on style conventions that have evolved in C programming. These conventions also suggest leaving a blank space between the keyword and the opening parenthesis. Some keywords, however, may not have parentheses following (for example, the `else` of an `if-else`).

A *function* consists of one or more statements designed to accomplish a small, specific task. A *function block* starts with the name of the function, followed by parentheses and then the opening brace. The `main()` function is an example.

```
main()
{
     ...
}
```

Note how the style of a function block differs from that of a statement block: the opening brace is placed below the first letter of the function name, and there is no space between the function name and the opening parenthesis. The opening and closing braces have the same alignment under the first letter of the function name.

Most C compilers include one or more files that contain a number of prewritten functions which can be used without modification in your programs.

1.2. The `main()` function is special for two reasons. First, this function marks the beginning and the end of a C program. Second, every C program must have a `main()` function to be able to execute the program. The shortest C program possible is

```
main()
{
}
```

This is called a *null program*. Obviously, this program doesn't do anything useful, but it is still a C program. Compiling a program like this, however, is not as stupid as it might seem. Because C compilers vary in quality, compiling such a program gives you some idea of the "overhead" that will be used with other useful C programs. I've seen one compiler that produces a null program that is as large as 10K—not very desirable.

1.3. A *library function* is any previously written function available for use in a program. The sample programs in the *Guide* and this book use the printf() function in most cases, but you are not required to write that function yourself. The programs work because someone wrote the printf() function and made it part of the function library. During the "link" phase of compiling a program (details are found in a later chapter), the linker searches the function library for any specified functions that are not written in the program itself. If the library contains the missing function, the linker merges it into the program. If the linker cannot find the function, the linker issues an error message.

The most likely reasons for this error message are that the missing function was not written, the name of the function was wrong, the function name was misspelled, the function was not in the supplied library, or the function was in a different library.

Try compiling the following program to discover the nature of the error message the linker gives you.

```
main()
{
       junk();
}
```

Unless your library contains a junk() function (highly unlikely), you should see an error message produced by the linker.

1.4. An *argument* is a piece of information that is passed to a function when the function is called. For example, suppose that you want to find out whether a character variable contains a digit (0 - 9). Most libraries contain a function called isdigit(), which is designed just for the purpose of getting that information. Obviously, isdigit() must "know" the character to be tested. If the character variable is named chr_test, the function call might look as follows:

```
main()
{
       . . .
       isdigit(chr_test);
       . . .
}
```

The name `chr_test` is the information the function `isdigit()` needs to perform its task: `chr_test` is the argument for the function call to `isdigit()`.

An *argument list* is used when the function requires more than one argument to perform its task. The example presented in figure 1.4 of the *Guide* contains a function that calculates the volume of a cube. Because three pieces of information are needed by the `volume()` function, it has an argument list containing three arguments.

Function arguments are often referred to as *function parameters,* or simply *parameters*. An argument list and a parameter list have identical meaning.

1.5. This is a trick question because there is currently no standard C library. The term *standard library* comes from the C language running under AT&T's UNIX operating system. The C standard library under UNIX is a set of libraries containing many different functions. However, parts of these libraries work with non-UNIX computers.

Outside UNIX, the C language does not specify what functions are to be available, because functions are not part of the language. In a strict sense, all compilers must provide for a `main()` function; otherwise, no program could be executed. Beyond that, whatever functions come with your compiler are "icing on the cake."

The concept of a standard library, however, is a brilliant idea. A standard library indicates not so much the content or depth of the library as that library functions behave in a consistent manner on all compilers. This consistency should extend to function name, argument (lists), and task. An example will help clarify the point.

Suppose that you want to use a function which copies a string variable. You need to know three things: the name of the function that will copy a string, the string that is to be copied, and where to put the copy of the string. Now suppose that one compiler writer calls the string copy function `s_copy()`, but another calls it `strcpy()`. Your program will compile on one compiler but not on the other (unless you change the function name). If the compiler writers agree on one name, however, your program is "portable": it can be compiled on either compiler without altering the source program file.

Even if the compiler writers agree on the same name, a problem can still exist. Suppose that you call the string to be copied *source* and the place to which it is to be copied destin (destination). The argument list for the function with one compiler is

    strcpy(source, destin);

and the other compiler uses

    strcpy(destin, source);

Although your program will compile with both compilers, your program will work correctly with only one compiler because the argument lists are reversed. The program under one compiler will copy the correct source string to the correct destination. But under the other compiler, nonsense will erupt when the program copies the incorrect source string (destin) to the incorrect destination string (source).

This type of confusion can be worse than having compilers that use different function names to do the same task. If the function names are different, both programs will compile, but the linker will issue an error message stating that a function is missing. This function is the one that has different names under the two compilers.

If the two compilers use the same function name but a different order for the function's argument, the program will compile and link under both compilers but only work correctly under one compiler. The task of debugging to find the "wrong function" is now left to you.

As this text is being written, an ANSI (American National Standards Institute) committee is working on standards for C. Most programmers probably hope that the committee will clear up some of the gray areas (for example, calling conventions for functions) but leave the essence of the language as it is.

The idea of a standard library, however, remains to provide consistency within the C function library across compilers. Ideally, a standard C function library would provide for all compilers functions that (1) use the same function names, (2) use the same order and number of arguments in the argument lists, and (3) perform tasks in identical ways.

1.6. Free form means that you can place C statements anywhere you wish without worrying about positional rules as long as the program conforms to the syntactic and semantic rules of C.

All languages have syntactic and semantic rules, and some have positional rules. For example, one dialect of BASIC requires that user-defined functions appear in the program before they are called. Generally, however, C does not have positional rules. You are free to put expressions, statements, blocks, and functions almost anywhere you want. Although there are some rules about the *sequence* of C statements (such as the need to declare a variable before you use it), you are free to put a statement anywhere. For example, a statement can be on the left or right margin of a line if even 50 blank lines fall between that statement and the next one.

As with any other freedom, there is a certain amount of responsibility. As you write more C programs, you will develop your own style. If you develop a style that is hard to read (particularly by others), don't expect too much help from colleagues when it comes time to debug your code. Most professional C programmers develop similar styles, especially if the programmers work together. Their styles are fundamentally the same although they may have some different nuances. I urge you to follow the tried-and-true style guidelines presented in Chapter 1 of the *C Programming Guide*. Throughout this self-study guide, additional style guidelines (not found in the *Guide*) will also be suggested.

1.7. The following data types are available:

```
char
int
float
double
```

In addition, the int data type can be preceded by the keywords short or long, and any int or char can be preceded by unsigned. The keyword float can be preceded by the word long, in which case long float is the same as a double. Therefore, you could add short int, long int, unsigned int, unsigned short int, unsigned long int, unsigned char, and long float to the preceding list.

Be aware that some compilers currently do not support several unsigned data types: unsigned char, unsigned short int, and unsigned long int. These are fairly new to C and are supported and used on UNIX System V.

The complete list is

```
char
     unsigned char
int
     short int
     long int
     unsigned int
     unsigned short int
     unsigned long int
float
     long float
double
```

The modifiers to the `int` data type can be used by themselves, and they usually are. The definitions

```
unsigned int x;
```

and

```
unsigned x;
```

are both correct, but the latter is used more often.

When you use two modifiers, their order does not matter. For example, `long unsigned int` is the same as `unsigned long int`.

Be cautious in using `long float`. It is an old data type that may be illegal someday. Use the `double` data type instead.

Some compilers do not support the `short`, `long`, `float`, or `double` data types. These compilers are called *subset compilers* because they do not support all C data types. So that you can get started in C with a minimum investment, the first five chapters of the *Guide* attempt to use only data types supported by subset compilers. The *Self-Study Guide*, however, assumes that you are working with a full C compiler (one that has all C data types and operators).

C has one more data type, which is called `void`. We'll discuss this data type in Chapter 3.

1.8. The data type `char` is defined as sufficient storage to hold one character of the character set used by the host computer. Most non-IBM mainframe computers use the ASCII character set, and for these computers one character is held in eight bits (one byte).

An `int` data type is defined as sufficient storage to hold an integer number used by the host computer. For most micro- and mini-computers, 16 bits are used for the integer data type. Because integer numbers can have negative values in C, the 16th bit is used for the sign, giving an integer a range from -32,768 to 32,767.

Larger machines based on a 32-bit architecture often use a signed 32-bit integer and have numbers ranging from -2,147,483,648 to 2,147,483,647. Therefore, the range an integer number can assume in C varies according to the "natural" word size of the host system.

(There are two accepted pronunciations for char: "char," as in something that is burned (the first part of *char*coal), and "care," as the first part of the word *char*acter. Because I cannot think of anything pleasant that is burned, I prefer the second pronunciation.)

1.9. The major problem with this program is that it will not run with most C compilers because the compiler does not know where to start the program. Upper- and lowercase letters are distinct in C. There is no main() function to begin the execution of the program because MAIN() and main() are not the same. BASIC programmers frequently make this mistake when they first start using C. They are not alone, however. I've seen programmers with years of experience try to use Main() with the same (nonexecuting) results. (This choice also was probably influenced by another language.)

These kinds of mistakes are common in the beginning, and you should not be discouraged by them. As you gain experience with C, these mistakes will disappear. (If you're like the rest of us, you'll move on to bigger and better ones!). Chapter 9 of the *Guide* points out some common mistakes and offers some suggestions for program debugging.

1.10. The general format for using printf() is

```
printf("control string", arg1, arg2, arg3, ...);
```

The control string often contains both English text and conversion characters. A conversion character, the percent sign (%), is immediately followed by the data type-specifier (and may include a field-width specification). For example, if you want to print a series of integers within a field of four spaces, you could use

```
printf("The answer is %4d and %4d", a, b);
```

Keep in mind that printf() is a powerful and therefore large function. Frequently, it has features that are not used but are included because those features are an inherent part of printf(). If you are using string constants only as output in a program, you can use the puts() function, which is used only for printing strings.

```
#include <stdio.h>

main()
{

    puts("This is my first C program.");
}
```

This version generates substantially less code than

```
#include <stdio.h>

main()
{

    printf("This is my first C program.\n");
}
```

because puts() does not have to cope with numeric data. The difference in code size is more dramatic on full compilers, where printf() must also handle long, float, and double data types.

The beginning line of the two programs

```
#include <stdio.h>
```

may be new to you. The purpose of this line is to include a file called stdio.h. For now, whenever you use a function like getchar(), putchar(), printf(), puts(), or gets(), you may need to have this line in your program. We'll explain more about #include and stdio.h later in this book.

1.11. First, you need to display numeric information, so printf() must be used. However, because printf() can also display character strings, the puts() function is not needed. If you change the puts()s to printf()s

```
printf("The purpose of this program is to add two\n");
printf("numbers together and display the results.\n");
```

the code size for the program should decrease because you have removed the puts() function. Note that you must add the newline character (\n) to the end of the printf() string for the output to be the same. puts() automatically adds a newline; printf() does not.

The point to remember is that if printf() is used in a program, there is no reason to call another function that duplicates some part of printf(). Likewise, if a program needs only one part of printf() (as in 1.10), there is probably another function in your library that will reduce code size.

Most compiler manufacturers will group the library functions by use (for example, input/output, string-character manipulation, etc.). Read the relevant sections of your compiler's documentation to get a feel for the functions at your disposal.

1.12. *Source code* is a humanly readable program written in the syntax of the language being used. An example of source code is the program in the previous answer. Source code programs are usually entered into the computer by some form of text editor or word processor.

Assembly code is a program that uses a set of abbreviations (or mnemonics) which reflect the instruction set used by the computer. For example, if instruction 195 of a computer causes the program to jump to a certain memory location, that instruction must be written in binary:

```
11000011
```

Humans don't relate to binary easily, so programmers have created assemblers that use abbreviations for the binary instructions. If programmers want to jump to memory location 0, they can write

```
JMP 0
```

instead of

```
11000011 00000000 00000000
```

Assembly code, therefore, is the form of a program that uses abbreviations (like JMP) for the actual binary instructions needed by the computer. Using these abbreviations (assembler language) is much easier than writing programs using numbers—especially binary numbers.

An *assembler* is a program that converts assembly language abbreviations into binary code. An assembler takes as its input an assembly language program (usually from a file stored on disk). The assembler transforms the instructions into either a directly executable program or an intermediate (that is, relocatable) form. Either product of the assembler is usually placed into a second disk file. Both of these forms are binary representations of the programs. The only difference is that one form can be used directly by the computer, whereas the intermediate form must go through another process before the computer can directly use the program. Most assemblers used with C compilers produce an intermediate form of a program.

Object code is either a program that is directly executable by the computer, or an intermediate form that is later transformed into a directly executable program. When most C programmers refer to object code, they are referring to this intermediate binary form.

A *linker* is a program that takes two or more binary subprograms (usually the intermediate form of a binary program) and links (or merges) them into one large executable program. For example, the source program in answer 1.11 uses two functions: `main()` and `printf()`. You have already seen that `printf()` is not in the program but is part of the standard library. The linker merges the binary code for the `printf()` function with the `main()` program. If the two functions are not linked, the program does not run properly.

Executable code is the the binary form of a program that can be executed directly by the computer. This binary program may have been the direct output of an assembler or C compiler, or may be the output of a linker.

A *librarian* is a program that lets you expand and maintain your library functions efficiently. The purpose of the librarian is best explained with an example.

Suppose that you have a written a file that has a function called `testit()`. You use `testit()` often in many of your programs. Whenever you write and compile a program that uses `testit()`, you must tell the linker to combine with your program the file holding `testit()`.

A librarian offers an alternative to telling the linker explicitly to combine `testit()` with your programs. Using a librarian, you can create a new library file containing `testit()`. Now you tell the linker to search the new library file holding `testit()` when you link any of your programs. If a program uses `testit()`, the linker will automatically add `testit()` to the program. If the program does not use `testit()`, the linker will skip this function and not add it to the program.

At this point, you have only replaced telling the linker to always add `testit()` to your program. You still must inform the linker that an additional library file must be searched. The real timesavings come when you create a library file holding many of your own functions. Now you simply tell the linker to search this new library file, and the linker will search and add only the functions used in your program.

You no longer need to specify the many additional files that hold these functions for the linker. One file fits all.

In essence, this is how the standard library that comes with your C compiler has been created. The compiler's author has individually written the functions in your library and, using a librarian, combined the functions into a library file. To include with your program any of the functions from your standard library, you simply tell the linker the name of this library file. The linker will search the library file and add the necessary individual functions to your finished program.

1.13. The example as presented is flawed. Because you used the %f conversion character in printf(), you want the program to treat the numeric constant 1 as a floating-point number. However, the compiler will not regard the constant as a floating-point number. (Given its value, the constant could be an int and will be made into an int data type by the compiler.) The error is not a syntactic error but a semantic one made by the programmer.

Semantic errors are errors that follow the syntactic rules but still don't behave correctly. The sentence, "The dog barked," follows the syntactic and semantic rules of English. The sentence, "The cat barked," follows the syntactic rules of English but not the semantic rules. The example in the preceding paragraph is a semantic error.

The correct way to inform the compiler that you wish to use a floating-point number is to use a decimal point (even though one may not be required) with all floating-point constants.

One correct way to code the program is to make the following change:

```
printf("A floating-point 1 is %f", 1.0);
```

In this way, the compiler senses that the constant is to be treated as a floating-point number. Even though this example is trivial, you should try both forms of the program with your compiler. I've seen results that range from printing a minus zero to locking up the computer.

Experimenting with known errors makes it easier to debug surprises later on. By observing the results of intentional bugs, you gain experience for detecting any unintentional bugs you may place in your programs.

1.14. The program is quite simple.

```
#include <stdio.h>

main()
{

        printf("\t+----+\n");
        printf("\t|    |\n");
        printf("\t|    |\n");
        printf("\t+----+\n");
}
```

2

Operators, Variables, and Loops

Questions about Operators, Variables, and Loops

2.1. What do the terms *operand* and *operator* mean in programming? How do they relate to the hierarchy of operators? *(Answer on p. 23.)*

2.2. What do the terms *unary operator*, *binary operator*, and *ternary operator* mean? *(Answer on p. 23.)*

2.3. What is the difference between an *arithmetic* and a *relational* operator? *(Answer on p. 24.)*

2.4. The first edition of the *Guide* presents only one form of the if-else statement, but this statement may be used another way. What are the two forms of this statement? *(Answer on p. 25.)*

2.5. Review the following program.

```
#include <stdio.h>

main()
{
    int i = 2;

    if (i == 1)
        printf("Monday\n");
    else if (i == 2)
        printf("Tuesday\n");
    else if (i == 3)
        printf("Wednesday\n");
    else if (i == 4)
        printf("Thursday\n");
    else if (i == 5)
        printf("Friday\n");
    else if (i == 6)
        printf("Saturday\n");
    else
        printf("Sunday\n");
}
```

What is printed on the console? Is *Sunday* printed in all cases? Why or why not? *(Answer on p. 26.)*

2.6. Write a program that accepts a number from the keyboard and then calls a function that returns the absolute value of the number. (Hint: Check your compiler documentation for the gets() and atoi() functions.) *(Answer on p. 27.)*

2.7. Write a program to demonstrate that preincrement and postincrement operators assign different values to a variable. *(Answer on p. 29.)*

2.8. What does a #define do, and how does it work? *(Answer on p. 30.)*

2.9. What is the advantage of using a #define in a program? *(Answer on p. 32.)*

2.10. If asked to write a program that squares an integer number, most people will simply multiply the number by itself and be done with it. Such an approach is rather dull, however; other algorithms (logs or addition, for example) can square a number.

One alternative is this: If x is the number to be squared, the sum of x odd integers starting with 1 gives the square of the number. That is, if x equals 3, the sum of the first 3 odd integers starting with 1 gives the square of x. Therefore, if x = 3

$$1 + 3 + 5 = \text{square}(3)$$

$$9 = 3 * 3$$

If x = 4:

$$1 + 3 + 5 + 7 = \text{square}(4)$$

$$16 = 4 * 4$$

Construct a program that squares a number by means of this algorithm. Try to use a while loop in the square function. *(Answer on p. 33.)*

2.11. What is the difference between a while and a do-while loop construct? *(Answer on p. 34.)*

2.12. Most for loops can be rewritten as while loops. What is the generalized form of a for loop written as a while loop? *(Answer on p. 34.)*

2.13. How can you write an infinite for loop? Are such loops actually useful in "real" programming? Are they good coding style? *(Answer on p. 37.)*

2.14. You already know what an integer data type is, and you should know the range of values the integer data type permits. How does the integer data type compare to the unsigned int data type? Is one more appropriate than the other in some instances? (Hint:

Read the paragraphs about the unsigned data type in Chapter 6 of the *Guide.*) *(Answer on p. 38.)*

2.15. Given the answer to 2.14, how would you modify the program in 2.10 to expand the range of numbers that can be processed? Does the program handle negative numbers in a graceful manner? *(Answer on p. 39.)*

2.16. In Appendix C, you will see an interesting and (perhaps useful) pattern. Can you determine the pattern? *(Answer on p. 41.)*

2.17. Assuming that you've answered 2.16, write a program that uses bit shifts to multiply and divide a number by 2. *(Answer on p. 42.)*

2.18. What is the difference between the *divide operator (/)* and the *modulus* or *modulo divide operator (%)* when the program is using integer data types? *(Answer on p. 43.)*

2.19. If a year is evenly divisible by 4 but not by 100, the year is a leap year. An exception is that years evenly divisible by 400 are leap years. Write a function that returns a value of 1 if the year is a leap year and 0 if it is not. *(Answer on p. 44.)*

2.20. Given the answer to 2.19, can you write the leap() in another form? *(Answer on p. 45.)*

2.21. Now that you have a leap() function, how would you use it in determining a Julian date? *(Answer on p. 46.)*

2.22. What is the difference between a break and a continue statement? *(Answer on p. 46.)*

2.23. Where does a break send program control in a nested while loop? *(Answer on p. 47.)*

2.24. What output is produced from the following program? *(Answer on p. 48.)*

```
#include <stdio.h>

#define MAXLOOP 10          /* Number of iterations */

main()
{
    int i;

    for (i = 0; i = MAXLOOP; ++i)
        printf("%d squared is %d\n", i, i * i);
}
```

Answers to Questions about Operators, Variables, and Loops

2.1. An *operand* is a variable or constant that is part of an expression. An *operator* tells which operation is to be performed on the operand(s). For example, the expression

```
c = a * b
```

has three operands (a, b, and c) and two operators: assignment (=) and multiplication (*).

The hierarchy of operators determines the order in which the operators perform their tasks on the operands. If you look at Appendix C, you will see that multiplication (number 4 on the list) has a higher ranking than assignment (number 14). Therefore, you know that the multiplication operator causes operands a and b to be multiplied before the result is assigned to c.

Programmers must pay close attention to the hierarchy of operators. For example, consider the following program:

```
main()
{
    int a, b, c, d;

    a = 2;
    b = 3;
    c = 4;

    d = a + b * c;

    printf("The result is %d", d);
}
```

Is the answer 20 or 14? The hierarchy of operators for the language determines the result to be 14. To change the way the expression is evaluated so that the answer is 20, you must use parentheses as follows:

```
d = (a + b) * c;
```

Because parentheses have higher ranking than the other operators, the operands a and b are added before the result is multiplied by c.

2.2. Each operator type refers to the number of operands needed for proper evaluation of the expression. For example, addition (+) is a *binary operator* because it requires two operands (variables, constants, or both) to perform its task. A *unary operator* needs only one operand, and a *ternary operator* requires three.

C provides all three types of operators, but you will be using binary most frequently. (The unary and ternary operators are discussed later in the book.)

2.3. An *arithmetic operator* uses its operands to produce a new, often intermediate, result. *Relational operators* compare two operands and decide whether the comparison is "logical" True or "logical" False, based on the relational operator used. Consider the following code fragment. (It is called a code fragment because it cannot be executed as written even though valid C syntax is used.)

```
int a, b, c;

a = 2;
b = 3;

c = a + b;                /* Arithmetic operation */

if (c > b)                /* Relational operation */
    printf("Relation is True");
else
    printf("Relation is False");
```

The arithmetic operation adds a and b to produce a result (5), which is then assigned to c. The relational operation that follows the addition [(c > b)] compares the value of c with the value of b and decides whether c is greater than (>) b. Because c is greater than b, the relation is logical True, and "Relation is True" is displayed on the console.

One more example will help establish the difference between arithmetic and relational operators.

```
int i, j, k;

j = 10;
k = 10;

i = j == k;               /* What is the result? */

printf("i = %d", i);
```

Because the relational operator for equality (==) has higher ranking than simple assignment (=), j is compared to k first. Because they are equal, the comparison evaluates the condition as logical True. A logical True in C evaluates to 1, so i is assigned the value 1.

If you change the value of either j or k so that the two do not have the same value, the relational test for equality becomes logical False and evaluates to zero, and i is assigned a value of 0. Although this example functions as described, the intention is clearer if you write

```
i = (j == k);
```

Arithmetic operators use their operands to produce some intermediate value that varies with the values of the operands. Relational operators compare their operands to produce a logical result of True (1) or False (0). Relational operations always evaluate to equal one of two values, 1 or 0, but arithmetic operations can evaluate to any number of values, depending on the operands themselves.

2.4. The formal statement of the if-else is

```
if (expression is logical True) {
    execute this statement(s);
} else {
    execute this statement(s);
}
```

If the expression within parentheses after the if is logical True, the statement(s) immediately following the expression is executed. If the expression is logical False, the statement(s) following the else is executed.

A second form of if-else deletes the keyword else. The following is also perfectly valid in C:

```
if (expression is logical True) {
    execute this statement(s);
}
```

This form of the if statement behaves as if the else controlled a null statement, a semicolon by itself. The lone if construct, therefore, is interpreted as though it were

```
if (expression is logical True) {
    execute this statement(s);
} else {
    ;                          /* A null statement */
}
```

Braces have been used in both examples to reinforce the fact that both `if` and `else` can control either a statement or a statement block. If an `if` or an `else` controls a single statement, the braces are normally omitted. When the `if` or `else` controls a statement block, braces must always be used. Forgetting the braces around a statement block is a common mistake for beginning C programmers.

Note that `else` can be used only with an `if`. You cannot use an `else` statement unless you have an `if` statement.

2.5. Because variable `i` is initialized to 2, *Tuesday* is printed on the console. *Sunday* is not printed. In programming parlance, Sunday is the *default* day because it is printed for any value of `i` other than 1 through 6. The program is a compound `if` statement. To reinforce what controls what, you can alter the form as follows:

```
#include <stdio.h>

main()
{
    int i = 2;

        if (i == 1)                         /* level 1 */
            printf("Monday\n");
        else if (i == 2)                    /* level 2 */
            printf("Tuesday\n");
        else if (i == 3)                    /* level 3 */
            printf("Wednesday\n");
        else if (i == 4)
            printf("Thursday\n");
        else if (i == 5)
            printf("Friday\n");
        else if (i == 6)
            printf("Saturday\n");
        else
            printf("Sunday\n");
}
```

If `i` equals 1 (the test at level 1), *Monday* is printed, and everything controlled by the corresponding `else` is ignored. In the example, all subsequent statements are ignored. If `i` equals 2, the expression (at level 1) `(i == 1)` is logical False, and the statement controlled by the `else` is executed. This statement is another `if` statement (at level 2). Because `i` now equals 2, the logical test (at level 2) on `(i == 2)` is logical True, and *Tuesday* is displayed. All subsequent lines are controlled by the next `else` and so would be evaluated only if the relational test (i == 2) were logical False. Therefore, when i equals 2, the rest of the program is not executed, and level 3 (and those following) is never reached.

With respect to coding style, the form presented in the question is a better choice than the one presented in this answer. As you will learn in a later chapter, however, C offers a better choice of syntax for handling the compound if construct, the switch statement. We'll discuss switch later in this book.

2.6. This answer employs functions from the standard library, with only a cursory explanation of what these functions do. They are discussed in detail later in the book. The following is one way the program can be written:

```
#include <stdio.h>

main()
{

        char string[20];
        int i;
        char *gets();

        printf("Enter an integer number: ");
        gets(string);          /* Get string from keyboard    */

        i = atoi(string);   /* Convert from ASCII to int    */
        i = abs(i);            /* Call absolute value function */

        printf("\n\nThe absolute value is: %d\n", i);
}


/*****
        Function to return the absolute value of an integer
        number. The value returned is an int data type.

        Argument list:    integer number x

        Return data type: integer

        CAUTION:          function cannot cope with unsigned or
                          floating-point data types
*****/

int abs(x)
int x;                          /* The positive or negative integer */
{
```

```
    if (x < 0)
        x = -x;

    return(x);
}
```

The program first defines several working variables. One is a character array called string[], which has 20 elements. Because C has no input/output words as part of the language, you must always get data as characters from the keyboard and then convert them to the data type you want.

After the variables are defined, the function gets() is declared to be a function that returns a pointer to char. We'll mention why this line is needed in the answer to question 2.15 later in this chapter.

The purpose of the gets() function is to take characters from the keyboard and place them in a character array. The function is called as gets(string), so the character array string[] is the argument to gets(). Every keystroke entered by the user is placed in string[]. The gets() function checks each keystroke to see whether it is a carriage return (the Return key or CR). When the function finds a CR, the program returns from gets() with the array containing the keystrokes entered plus another character that will be discussed shortly.

For example, if you enter the number -45, the string[] array looks as follows (assuming that it was placed in memory location 50,000):

50000   50019

| - | 4 | 5 | \0 | | | |

There are several important things to notice in the diagram. First, even though string[] is capable of holding 20 characters, only 4 elements are used. The remaining elements are still available. How does C determine where the string of characters ends? C determines the end of the string (or EOS) by sensing the \0 character at the end of the string. This special character is called the *null character*, also called a *null*.

How did the null character get placed at the end of the string? You didn't enter it from the keyboard. The gets() entered the null when the function sensed the CR you entered when you pressed Return. The program uses the CR to determine when you finish entering the characters and substitutes a null for the CR so that the compiler senses where your string entry ends. The compiler reads the characters only to the null and does not consider the remaining (empty) characters of string[].

Because string[] is a character array, you cannot treat the contents of the array as a number. You must convert the array from a string of characters to an integer value. The atoi() function is designed to perform ASCII-to-integer conversions. To do this, atoi() needs to "know" the character array that contains what you entered. Therefore, the argument to the atoi() is the string[] character array. When the atoi() is finished, it returns an integer value that is then assigned to variable i. Now that i is an integer value, you can call your own function, which returns the absolute value of i.

Note the style used in the comments that precede the actual code for the function. The style shown is not etched in stone; but you should always tell the reader what the function does, what is the nature of any arguments used by the function, what is returned from the function, and perhaps what might cause the function to "blow up."

The abs() function simply checks the value of the argument provided. The function checks variable x to see if its value is less than zero. If so, the if test (x < 0) is logical True, and x is assigned the numerically opposite value of x, which changes x into a positive number. If x starts as a positive number, the if test is logical False, and the value is returned unchanged. The program then assigns the value returned from abs() to variable i and displays the result.

Experienced C programmers probably do not code main() as it is presented here. Rather, they combine the calls to gets() and atoi() in the following manner:

```
i = atoi(gets(string));
```

If you want to modify the program to this form, consult your compiler's documentation to determine why the function still works as before.

2.7. The program is self-explanatory.

```
#include <stdio.h>

main()
{
        int i, j;

        i = 99;

        printf("The value of i is %d\n", i);

        j = ++i;

        printf("\nFirst a preincrement on i\n");
        printf("The value of j = %d and i = %d\n", j, i);

        i = 99;

        printf("\nThe value of i is now %d again\n", i);

        j = i++;

        printf("\nHaving done a postincrement on i\n");
        printf("j = %d and i = %d\n", j, i);
}
```

The same general form can be used also to verify how the pre- and postdecrement (--) operators work.

2.8. The #define is actually a preprocessor directive, not a keyword. (See table 1.1 in the *Guide* to verify that #define is not a keyword in C.) To understand fully what a #define is, you must understand what the macro preprocessor pass does to the source code of a program.

The preprocessor pass is the first pass the compiler makes when compiling a program. This pass examines the C source code for preprocessor directives, of which #define is one it recognizes. Assume, for example, that the source program contains the following lines:

```
#define BELL 7           /* Line 1              */
    ...                  /* Other program lines */
printf("%c", BELL);      /* Line 50             */
    ...                  /* More program lines  */
```

When the preprocessor reads line 1 in the program, the preprocessor looks in memory—at a place it has created and named the macro symbol table—to see whether BELL has been defined for this program. Because this is the first line of the program, the preprocessor cannot find BELL in the macro symbol table, so the preprocessor enters BELL with the associated number 7 in the macro symbol table.

If a later line in the program (say, line 30) contains a second #define BELL 7, the preprocessor pass looks for BELL in the macro symbol table. Because BELL is already in the macro symbol table, the preprocessor issues an error message. The exact wording varies among compilers, but it is something like "Symbol BELL multiply defined." Therefore, each #define in a program must be unique from all others in the same program.

Eventually, the preprocessor pass reads line 50 and finds

```
printf("%c", BELL);      /* Line 50 */
```

The preprocessor again looks in the macro symbol table to see whether BELL is defined for the program. Because BELL is in the macro symbol table, the preprocessor takes whatever has been defined to be BELL (7 in this example) and replaces BELL with its definition. As a result, when the preprocessor finishes line 50, it's as if the line read

```
printf("%c", 7);      /* Line 50 */
```

When the next pass of the compiler converts the program, the compiler "knows" that you want to print an ASCII 7 at line 50 of the program. Appendix C indicates that an ASCII 7 sounds the bell on the terminal. Therefore, when line 50 is executed during a run of the program, you will hear the terminal's bell.

The purpose of a #define, therefore, is to signal the preprocessor pass of the compiler to make a text replacement of a symbolic constant that has been #defined in the program. According to the following definition,

```
#define  symbolic constant   text replacement
```

a #define takes a *symbolic constant* (for example, BELL) and replaces it with the *text replacement* (7) everywhere the symbolic constant occurs in the program.

Clearly, a #define of a symbolic constant must occur before the symbolic constant can be used in the program. Otherwise, the compiler issues an error message like "variable undefined," because the symbolic constant has not been defined in the macro symbol table.

2.9. Suppose that you use a #define to define the clear screen code for your CRT or video screen. Further assume that your clear screen code is an ASCII Escape followed by an ASCII asterisk (*). In Appendix C, you find that an Escape code is a decimal 27, or 033 in octal. The clear screen code consists of two ASCII characters, so you must treat the clear screen codes as a string constant. Therefore, the correct #define is

```
#define CLEAR   "\033*"
```

The leading backslash within a string constant tells the compiler that what follows is a single ASCII character. The character is presented, in this example, in octal as the number for the ASCII character. Because 033 in octal is an ASCII Escape, the Escape character appears in the string constant at the place where you see the \033 in the string constant. You must use the backslash followed by the octal representation of the ASCII character because an Escape is a nonprinting ASCII character.

Now suppose that you use the symbolic constant CLEAR at 30 different places in the program. After the preprocessor pass of the compiler, you might find 30 instances of

```
printf(CLEAR);
```

This statement causes the preprocessor to substitute

```
printf("\033*");
```

When the program is run, each occurrence of printf(CLEAR) causes the CRT to clear the screen.

Now consider what will happen if you do not use a #define for the clear screen codes. In this case, you will type 30 occurrences of

```
printf("\033*");
```

If your life is like mine, the day after you finish the program, your boss will bring in a new CRT or video screen for you. Invariably, the clear screen codes are different for the new terminal. Therefore, you now have to go into the source code, find and change the 30 different places where the clear screen codes appear, and then recompile the program.

If you use a #define, however, you change only the #define in the source code of the program. When the program is recompiled, the preprocessor automatically changes the 30 occurrences of the clear screen codes.

For example, the new CLEAR for any terminal that uses the ANSI standard control code is

```
#define CLEAR "\033[2J"
```

By changing this single line and recompiling, you can use the program with any ANSI terminal or display.

Liberal use of #defines for program constants can reduce the time required for program changes if the constants change in the future (which they always seem to do). The use of #defines also makes it easier to move from one hardware environment to another; thus, #defines make the code more portable.

2.10. One possibility might be

```
#include <stdio.h>

#define MAXINT  179           /* Largest integer that's safe */

main()
{
        char string[20];
        int i;
        char *gets();

        printf("Enter a positive integer number: ");
        i = atoi(gets(string));

        printf("\nThe square of %d is %d\n", i, square(i));
}

/*****
        Function to square an integer value

        Argument list:    integer number value

        Return data type: integer

        CAUTION:          function cannot cope with integer
                          values greater than MAXINT
*****/

int square(value)
int value;
{
```

```
        int bump = 1,  sum = 0;

        if (value > MAXINT)
                printf("number too large to square");
        else
                while (value--) {
                        sum = sum + bump;
                        bump = bump + 2;
                }

        return(sum);
}
```

Why does the program use a #define on MAXINT? The size of an integer data type may differ on different computers used to run the program. Most computers define an integer to be 16 bits, but some have integers with 32 bits. This program assumes that an integer contains 16 bits. If you want to move to a computer that uses 32-bit integers, you simply change the value associated with MAXINT to the value 46,339. Even if you don't change MAXINT, the function still works on the larger machine.

The code in main() is similar to that presented in 2.6. Note one thing, however, about the way the square() function is written. It could have been written as

```
if (value > MAXINT) {
        printf("number too large to square");
        return(0);              /* return no. 1 */
}

while (value--) {
        sum = sum + bump;
        bump = bump + 2;
}

return sum;                     /* return no. 2 */
```

If you write the function in the latter form, there are two places from which you can exit from the function (return numbers 1 and 2). Experience suggests that functions with only one exit point (only one return statement) are easier to debug and maintain than those with multiple exit points. Therefore, the second alternative is less desirable because it has multiple exit points (two return statements), whereas the first solution has a single exit point. Whenever possible, write functions that use a single return statement.

One final point: How does the while (value--) terminate the loop? A while loop continues to execute as long as the expression controlling the loop remains logical True. At some point, value is decremented to zero. When this occurs, the expression becomes logical False because 0 is the number associated with logical False.

2.11. The difference is the point at which the test occurs in determining whether to execute the loop. Consider the following code fragment:

```
int i = 1,  j = 2,  sum = 0;

do {
      sum = i + j;        /* statement(s) of do-while */
} while (i == j);

sum = 0;
while (i == j)
      sum = i + j;        /* statement(s) of while    */
```

Both loops have the same test condition: i == j. When the do-while is executed, sum equals 3 by the time the while is tested, because there is *always* one pass through the statement(s) controlled by a do-while loop. Because i does not equal j, the test is logical False, and no more passes are made through the do-while. As a result, sum equals 3.

On the other hand, sum equals 0 after the simple while loop. The test on i and j is made *before* the statements controlled by the while are executed. Because no passes are made through the statement(s) controlled by the while loop, sum exits from the loop with a value of 0.

As a final point, the braces are not needed in the preceding do-while loop because only one statement is being controlled by the loop. The braces, however, were included because they help to identify the do-while loop. Indeed, I know of one popular C compiler that cannot compile a program without braces in a do-while. (Possibly, the programmer felt that do-while loops always control a statement block and forced you to use braces, or perhaps a bug is lurking in that compiler. Take your pick.)

2.12. The general forms of the for and while loops are

```
for (expression 1; expression 2; expression 3)
      statement;
```

and

```
while (expression)
        statement;
```

To convert a for loop into a while loop, the generalized form is

```
expression 1;
while (expression 2) {
        statement(s);
        expression 3;
}
```

For example, given the following code fragment of a for loop (assume all variables have been declared properly),

```
for (i = 0, sum = 0; i < 100; ++i)
    sum = sum + i;
```

the same code fragment expressed as a while loop becomes

```
i = 0;
sum = 0;
while (i < 100 ) {
    sum = sum + i;
    ++i;
}
```

Note that expression 1 of the for loop contains two subexpressions (i = 0 and sum = 0) separated by a comma. The comma is used to separate subexpressions within a larger expression. If this is true, can you write the while as in the following?

```
i = 0,                  /* Note the comma, not semicolon */
sum = 0;
while (i < 100 ) {
    sum = sum + i;
    ++i;
}
```

Try this version to see what happens on your compiler.

Because C permits variables of the same data type to be initialized at one time,

```
i = sum = 0;
```

is valid in C. Therefore, the for can also be written as

```
for (i = sum = 0; i < 100 ; ++i)
```

This form relates more directly to the while

```
i = sum = 0;              /* expression 1 */
while (i < 100) {         /* expression 2 */
    sum = sum + i;
    ++i;                  /* expression 3 */
}
```

The choice of a for or a while usually makes no difference.

2.13. An infinite for loop has the form

```
for (; ;) {
    statement(s);
}
```

Perhaps more important is the question of why the loop behaves as an infinite loop? The full form is

```
for (expression 1; expression 2; expression 3)
    statement;
```

where

expression 1 is usually one or more initializer expressions
(e.g., i = 0).

expression 2 performs some logical test on the expression
(e.g., i < 100).

expression 3 usually is an increment expression
(e.g., ++i)

expression 2, therefore, determines when the loop actually terminates. The proper way to view a for (; ;) statement is as a for in which all three expressions are null statements. Because there is nothing in expression 2 to terminate the loop and you can execute null statements forever, an infinite for loop is created.

Infinite loops, of course, are useful, provided some mechanism is included to break out of the loop. The fragments presented in figures 2.15, 2.16, and 2.17 of the *Guide* are examples. Infinite loop constructs, therefore, normally contain a break statement somewhere within the loop. That is, you would expect to see something like

```
for (; ;) {
    . . .
    if (expression)
        break;
    . . .
}
```

somewhere within the loop. When the expression controlled by the if evaluates to logical True, the program breaks out of the infinite loop.

Most programmers prefer to write infinite loops in another form. A common style is

```
#define TRUE 1
    . . .

    . . .
while (TRUE) {
    . . .
    if (expression)
        break;
    . . .
}
    . . .
```

This form creates an infinite loop that is more recognizable as such. A #define defines the symbolic constant TRUE with a value of 1. After the preprocessor pass, the while loop appears as while(1), which is always logical True, and thus creates an infinite loop.

Although the code generated by the compiler is probably the same with the for or the while infinite loops, the while construct may be the better choice because the intention is clearer.

2.14. There is a reason for skipping to Chapter 6 to introduce the unsigned int data type. First, both the unsigned int and the int data types are usually stored as 16-bit numbers (32-bit numbers on 32-bit computers). However, because an unsigned int does not consider the sign of the number, it has a range of values (0 through 65,535 for 16-bit integers, 0 through 4,294,967,295 for 32-bit integers) that is much larger than that of the integer data type. Second, most computers are more efficient when comparing unsigned numbers than when comparing signed numbers.

These two facts suggest that the unsigned int is often a better choice for variables used to control loops. In many cases, variables within loops will assume only positive values; these variables might benefit by being made the unsigned int data type. A judicious choice of unsigned int may lessen code size and execution time. (The issues of code size and execution speed will be addressed again in the section about storage class.)

2.15. One possible solution is

```
#include <stdio.h>

#define MAXINT  255        /* Largest integer that's safe */
                           /* yet bigger than plain int */


main()
{
        char string[20];
        int i;
        char *gets();
        unsigned int square();                    /* Strange !? */

        printf("Enter an integer number: ");
        i = atoi(gets(string));

        printf("\nThe square of %d is %u\n", i, square(i));
}


/*****
        Function to square an integer value

        Argument list:    integer number value

        Return data type: unsigned integer

        CAUTION:          function cannot cope with integer
                          values greater than MAXINT
*****/

unsigned int square(value)
int value;
{
        unsigned int bump = 1, sum = 0;

        if (value < 0)
                value = -value;

        if (value > MAXINT)
                printf("number too large to square");
        else
                while (value--) {
                        sum = sum + bump;
                        bump = bump + 2;
                }

        return(sum);
}
```

The first thing to consider is the use of the `unsigned int` data type to extend the range of values that can be processed. Using `unsigned int` permits you to extend MAXINT to 255. In doing so, however, you gain a new responsibility.

Recall that the integer data type is the default value returned from a function. The problem is that you want your `square()` function to return an answer that is an `unsigned int` rather than an `int`. Because you call `square()` from `main()`, `main()` is going to "think" that `square()` is passing back an `int` unless you specify otherwise. This is the purpose of the

```
unsigned int square();
```

declaration that appears near the beginning of `main()`. Such a declaration overrides the default return data type from a function call, and `main()` recognizes that `square()` returns an `unsigned int` data value.

Because the answer from `square()` may well exceed the value of a simple `int`, you must also change `printf()` to print an `unsigned int` value. This change means using the %u conversion character within `printf()`.

Now look at the first line of the `square()` function:

```
unsigned int square(value)
```

To design a function that returns an `unsigned int` value, place the return data type before the function name. The functions that return integer values do not require the word `int` because `int` is the default value. Therefore, the general form for the first line of a function definition should have three parts:

```
return data type    function_name(argument list)
     (1)                  (2)            (3)
```

This subject is discussed further in Chapter 3.

Once inside the definition of `square()`, you declare bump and sum to be `unsigned int` data types because you want to deal with larger numbers than `int` allows. Next, check to see whether value is a negative number. Because any number times itself is positive, use the unary minus operator (logical negation) to convert value to a positive number if it is negative.

The rest of the program operates as it did before.

We declared that `square()` returns an `unsigned int` in `main()` because `square()` returns a type other than an `int`. We have been declaring gets() in main() for the same reason. gets() returns a pointer to char. If this declaration is not made, the compiler believes that gets() returns an int.

Notice, however, that atoi() expects a string (actually a pointer to char) as its argument. Strange and unpredictable things may happen as the char * from gets() is tranformed to an int and given to atoi(). For example, all compilers will compile without error a program with a missing char *gets() declaration; however, the compiled program may work with some compilers but not with others. This result, if it should happen, is due to differences in compilers. However, the problem is not in the compiler but with the programmer, who is responsible for declaring functions that return a data type other than an int.

If in doubt about this rule, be safe and declare the function.

2.16. Consider how the compiler sees the following decimal numbers.

decimal	binary
1	0000000000000001
2	0000000000000010
4	0000000000000100
8	0000000000001000
16	0000000000010000

With the help of Appendix C, you can extend this chart to decimal 128. Multiplying by 2 causes a shift left of one bit position. For example, decimal 10 in binary is

0000000000001010

Multiplying by 2 gives decimal 20. In binary (see Appendix A) this is

0000000000010100

Therefore, when you shift all the bits in an integer one position to the left, you are multiplying the number by 2. Likewise, when you shift the bits one position to the right, you are dividing the number by 2.

Could this be useful? Perhaps. Many computers (especially 8-bit machines) can do bit shifting more quickly than multiplication.

Does C provide such bit shifting? Yes. The movements are logical operations and use the following operators:

$\ll n$ shift left *n* bit positions

$\gg n$ shift right *n* bit positions

For example, to shift a bit one position to the left and assign it to a variable, use

```
i = i << 1;
```

There is one "gotcha" associated with the use of bit shifts, however: they don't pay attention to the sign bit used in integer numbers. For example, the largest positive value for an integer number is 32,767, which is

011111111111111

in binary. On the other hand, a negative value in binary turns on the most significant bit (MSB). Therefore, multiplying 32,767 by 2 gives

┌─Most Significant Bit (MSB)
│
↓

111111111111110

which is interpreted as a negative number.

This problem disappears, however, if the variable used is an `unsigned int` data type, because the sign bit (MSB) is ignored. Therefore, you can use this technique safely with only the `unsigned int` data type.

This is not a new discovery, of course. Indeed, most commercial C compilers use bit shifts to optimize multiplying by two and dividing by two. However, because of the sign-bit problem, these optimizers can operate only when the `unsigned int` data type is used. This is yet another reason for using the `unsigned int` data type wherever possible.

2.17. Consider the following example:

```
#include <stdio.h>

main()
{
        unsigned i;

        i = 500;

        printf("i = %u\n", i);
        i = i << 1;                  /* First shift */
```

```
    printf("i = %u after shift left 1 position\n", i);

    i = i >> 2;                    /* Second shift */

    printf("i = %u after shift right 2 positions\n", i);
}
```

Because i is an unsigned int, the %u conversion character must be used in all the printf()s. Variable i is assigned a value of 500 and then shifted one position to the left. The net result of the first shift is the same as that from multiplying by 2.

The second bit-shift operation shifts right 2 bit positions, the same as dividing by 4. The result of this operation yields an answer of 250.

If you're so inclined, you might recode this program to use a "multiply by 2" and then a "divide by 4" to see whether the assembler code produced by the compiler is the same in both cases. If they are, the compiler implements the bit-shift optimizer mentioned in 2.16.

2.18. Suppose you have the following code fragment:

```
int i;

i = 5;

printf("i = %d\n", i / 2);

printf("i = %d\n", i % 2);
```

What is produced on the console? The first printf() does an integer divide, which produces i = 2. Integer division ignores (truncates) any remainder of the division.

On the other hand, the second printf() does a modulo divide, which produces i = 1. The modulus is the *remainder* of the division. Modulo division behaves as if you subtracted the divisor from the number until the next subtraction would produce a negative answer. That is,

```
5 - 2 = 3
3 - 2 = 1      /* Stop because next answer is negative */
1 - 2 = -1
```

This is the same as a remainder of 1. It is incorrect to use the modulus operator on floating-point numbers.

The expression *5 % 2* normally is verbalized as "five mod 2." (After all, you want to sound good the next time this topic comes up at a cocktail party, right?)

2.19. This question tests your ability to implement a function from a verbal description of the algorithm. It also gives you some practice using logical operators. A program using the function follows.

```
#include <stdio.h>

main()
{
        char string[20];
        int year;
        char *gets();

        printf("Enter a year: ");
        year = atoi(gets(string));

        printf("\n\n%d is ", year);

        if (!leap(year))
                printf("not ");

        printf("a leap year.\n");
}


/*****
        Function to determine if a year is a leap year

        Argument list: integer value for year

        Return value: 1 if it is a leap year, 0 if not

        CAUTION:        none
*****/

int leap(year)
int year;
{       int i = 0;
        if (year % 4 == 0 && year % 100 != 0 || year % 400 == 0)
                i = 1;
        return (i);
}
```

The program first gets the year from the user and then calls the leap() function as part of an if statement.

```
if (!leap(year))
    printf("not ");
```

What does the preceding function do? First, the leap() function is called with year as its argument. The return value from leap() will be 1 or 0. If the value is 1, the if views the return value as logical True. However, because you placed a logical *not* (!) operator in front of the call to leap(), you reverse the logic. That is, if 0 (logical False) is returned from leap(), the if sees it as logical True. (The 0 is now a 1.) If you don't have a leap year, the returned value is 0, which becomes a 1 by the logical *not*, and the program prints the word not on the CRT.

An alternative is

```
printf("\n\n%d ", year);
if (leap(year))
    printf("is");
else
    printf("is not");

printf(" a leap year.\n");
```

This function preserves the return logical from leap() but is somewhat longer.

The leap() function should look fairly straightforward to you although it has a number of logical operators. Verify that it follows the verbal description of the algorithm.

2.20. Try replacing

```
if (year % 4 == 0 && year % 100 != 0 || year % 400 == 0)
```

in the leap() function with

```
if ( !(year % 4) && (year % 100) || !(year % 400) )
```

Convince yourself that the logical of the algorithm presented in 2.19 is preserved.

As a nested question, are all the parentheses in the alternative specification necessary? If not, which ones are not needed? (Hint: Compare the hierarchy of the logical *not* operator with that of the modulus operator. What happens to year in some cases?)

Finally, if you've already read the *Guide*, use a ternary operator in the leap() function.

2.21. Professors tend to ask open-ended questions, and this is an example. This question does, however, ask you to think about an easy way to handle leap years.

A Julian date determines the number of days between two dates. Obviously, you need to account for leap years. Somewhere in your code, you probably have an array called `months[]`, which has been initialized to the number of days in the specified month. For example, `month[1]` equals 31, `month[2]` 28, and so on. Another variable (x) is used to index into (pick the correct member from) the `month[]` array. (In this case, you may want to initialize `month[0]` to 365 and begin the actual months with element 1 of the array to simplify indexing into the array.)

With this approach, dealing with leap years becomes a fairly painless single `if-else` statement:

```
if (x == 2)
     days = days + month[2] + leap(year);
else
     days = days + month[x];
```

The statement takes the current value of `days`, adds 28 plus the return value from `leap()`, which is 1 if the year is a leap year, but 0 otherwise. Therefore, if the year is a leap year, the statement reduces to

```
if (x == 2)
     days = days + 28 + 1;
```

or 29 days in February for a leap year.

2.22. The purpose of a `break` is to transfer program control out of the controlling `while`, `do-while`, `for`, or `switch` statement. (The `switch` statement is discussed later.) The purpose of a `continue` statement is to transfer program control to the next iteration of the same loop.

A diagram may help illustrate the difference.

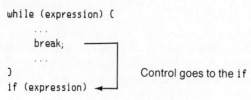

```
while (expression) {
     . . .
     break;
     . . .
}                        Control goes to the if
if (expression)
     . . .
```

When a continue is used

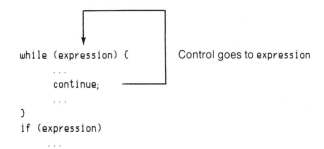

```
while (expression) {
    . . .
        continue;
    . . .
}
if (expression)
    . . .
```

Control goes to expression

In both cases, the lines of code following the break or continue within the while loop are ignored. Therefore, a break sends you completely out of the loop, but a continue does the next iteration of the same loop.

2.23. A break sends program control out of the innermost loop containing the break statement. For example,

```
while (TRUE) {                /* start main loop    */
    . . .
    while (j < MAXVAL) {      /* start second loop */
        . . .
        if (x == MAXVAL)
            break;            /* first break        */
        . . .
    }                         /* end (j < MAXVAL)   */
    if (time == QUIT)
        break;                /* second break       */
    . . .
}                             /* end (TRUE)         */
printf("End\n");
```

The first break, which is executed when x equals MAXVAL, sends control to the if (time == QUIT) statement, not the printf(). When time equals QUIT, the program exits from the second break, which sends program control out of the infinite while (TRUE) loop to the printf().

A break statement sends program control out of the loop structure that contains the break. It does *not* send program control out of every controlling loop structure. For instance, it will not send you from the first break to the printf().

Finally, notice how comments were used to mark the end of each while loop. Although comments are not much needed in this simple example, they are useful in large loops that span several pages.

2.24. When you typed the program, were you surprised by the output? The program produces an infinite loop that prints out

```
10 squared is 100
```

forever. Why?

The reason is that you used the assignment operator (=) in expression 2 of the for loop:

```
i = MAXLOOP              /* This is expression 2 */
```

This operator sets i equal to 10 for the loop. Because i is a nonzero value, the result of the assignment is nonzero. As C treats expression 2 as a relational test, the relational test in this example is always logical True. After the printf() is executed, i is incremented to 11. However, because you then evaluate expression 2 of the for loop, i is reassigned to 10.

Every C programmer should expect a fair share of this kind of error. Just bear in mind that expression 2 of a for loop performs a logical test, not an assignment.

3
Writing Functions

Questions about Writing Functions

3.1. What is a type-specifier in C? *(Answer on p. 53.)*

3.2. Why are type-specifiers important in C? *(Answer on p. 53.)*

3.3. Is there any way to reduce the chance of using a function in an assignment when nothing useful is returned from that function? (See 3.2 before answering.) *(Answer on p. 54.)*

3.4. What are *argument lists* and *argument declarations*? *(Answer on p. 55.)*

3.5. What are common mistakes and misconceptions about argument lists and declarations? *(Answer on p. 56.)*

3.6. I've heard other C programmers use the term *function parameters*, but not function arguments. What's the difference? *(Answer on p. 57.)*

3.7. What is meant by the terms *storage class* and *scope* in C? *(Answer on p. 57.)*

3.8. How does the storage class of a variable affect the way the compiler treats the variable? *(Answer on p. 61.)*

3.9. The following function presents one version of the sieve of Eratosthenes, which has often been used as a benchmark for the performance of C compilers. The purpose of the benchmark is to see how efficiently the compiler uses automatic variables. Enter the program and then time how long it takes to execute on your machine. Having done that, modify the program to take advantage of some of the ideas presented in this text. What happens to your time? *(Answer on p. 62.)*

```
/* Christopher Kern, January, 1983, BYTE */

#include <stdio.h>

#define TRUE    1
#define FALSE   0
#define SIZE 8190

char        flags[SIZE+1];
```

```
main()
{
        int i, prime, k, count, iter;

        printf("10 iterations.\n");
        for (iter = 1; iter <= 10; iter++){
                count = 0;
                for (i = 0; i <= SIZE; i++)
                        flags[i] = TRUE;
                for (i = 0; i <= SIZE; i++){
                        if (flags[i]){
                                prime = i + i + 3;
                                for (k = i + prime; k <= SIZE;
                                        k += prime)
                                                flags[k] = FALSE;
                                count++;

                        }
                }
        }
        printf("%d %d\n", prime, count);

}
```

3.10. The answer in 3.9 seems to be a strong argument for declaring all variables of the external storage class. Is this correct? *(Answer on p. 63.)*

3.11. Is there any way to gain the more efficient addressing of variables with the external storage class and still maintain the degree of privacy afforded by automatic variables? *(Answer on p. 64.)*

3.12. Variables with the automatic storage class are limited to the block in which they are defined. How can they be used in other functions that need them? *(Answer on p. 64.)*

3.13. What is an exception to the privacy afforded to variables of the automatic and internal static storage classes? *(Answer on p. 65.)*

3.14. Other than changing the storage class of the variables, in what ways can a program's performance be improved? *(Answer on p. 66.)*

3.15. Suppose that you are designing a large program that will consist of a main() file and five supporting files which are to be linked into the main() file. Each file must refer to a list of ten variables of the external storage class, defined in `main()`. How would you declare these variables in each file? *(Answer on p. 67.)*

3.16. Write a function that will convert a decimal number to the same number for any base 2 through 16. *(Answer on p. 69.)*

3.17. How important is the design phase in producing a working program? *(Answer on p. 70.)*

3.18. Question 2.9 in the previous chapter suggested that symbolic constants be used for the clear screen codes for the CRT. What is an alternative that preserves those advantages but offers an additional advantage? *(Answer on p. 71.)*

Answers to Questions
about Writing Functions

3.1. A type-specifier is part of a function definition that tells what data type is returned from the function. For example, figure 3.2 in the *Guide* shows a simple function that cubes a number. The first line of the function definition is

```
int cube(number)
```

In this example, int is the type-specifier for the function cube(). By looking at the type-specifier, we know that this function returns an int data type to whatever called cube().

3.2. Type-specifiers tell you what type of data is returned when the function is executed. They also can lead to a common cause of bugs in C programs, especially for the beginner.

The default type-specifier for a function definition in C is the int data type. You could also define the cube() function in figure 3.2 as

```
cube(number)
```

The C compiler would correctly process the function and return an int to whatever called cube().

The type-specifier is important, however, for two reasons. First, data types other than int can be returned by a function. Second, not all functions return something useful. If you write a function with this line

```
return;
```

or write the function with no return statement, "integer-sized junk" is returned from the function. To illustrate this point further, consider the following:

```
main()
{
    int i;
        . . .
    i = func();
}
func()
{
    . . .        /* A function body with no return */
    . . .        /* statement                      */
}
```

Where's the problem? Because func() does not use a return(*expression*) statement, the programmer has no idea what will be returned from the function. To complicate matters, whatever is returned from func() (and something *will* be returned) has been assigned into i in main(). As garbage is returned from func(), the error is easy to detect. Yet Murphy's law continues to "reign supreme," and it will probably take a long time to figure out what went wrong in this program.

Whenever you write a new function, do *not* rely on the default type-specifier. Always write the type-specifier as part of the function definition even though the function returns an int. Developing the habit of designating type-specifiers will help prevent errors when you write functions that return data types other than int.

3.3. A new data type, void, has been added to C on UNIX System V. void is a typeless data type. When used in a function definition, void tells the compiler that the function returns nothing useful. For example, notice the following:

```
void func()
{
     . . .
}
```

By defining func() as void, we tell the compiler that func() returns nothing useful and tell ourselves that the return value of func() should not be used in any calculation or assignment.

Many microcomputer C compilers do not treat void as a keyword. If your compiler does not support this convention, you can still use it. Simply use a #define statement at the beginning of your program in the following manner:

```
#define void int
     . . .
main()
{
     . . .
     void func();
     . . .
     func();
     . . .
}
void func()
{
     . . .
}
```

The preprocessor changes the word void to int so that the program can be compiled successfully, but void remains in the source code to remind you not to use func() in an assignment. If your compiler treats void as a keyword, simply remove the #define void int line from your program.

On compilers that do treat void as a keyword, you must declare void functions before you use them. A function that returns void returns a value other than an int, even if the value is no value. If you don't declare void functions beforehand, you will get an error message like "function redefinition." Note that if your compiler does not treat void as a keyword, you should nevertheless declare the function. You will be able to convert your programs with minimal fuss when your compiler respects the void keyword.

3.4. An *argument list* contains the names of any variables, otherwise unavailable, that the function needs to complete its task. In the cube() function, for example, number is the name of the variable to be cubed; it is the argument list for cube().

To complete its task, not every function needs information. For instance, getchar(), the function that gets a single character from the keyboard, does not use an argument list. You do not place any variable in between the parentheses for getchar(). Therefore, the argument list of a function can be empty or contain as many arguments as the function needs to complete its task.

If a function requires an argument list, the function also needs an *argument declaration*. An argument declaration tells the function the data type of each variable in the argument list. For example, if a function needs to know the character (c) just typed by the user and its position (position) in a line on the CRT or screen, the function definition might be

```
void crt_loca(position, c)   /* No semicolon    */
int  position;               /* Argument decla #1 */
char c;                      /* Argument decla #2 */
{
       . . .

}
```

The argument list (position, c) is always enclosed by parentheses and immediately follows the function name (crt_loca). This is a function definition; it is not a statement and therefore should not have a semicolon at the end of the line. The argument declaration(s) appears after the argument list but before the opening brace of the function body.

Because the default data type in C is int, you can define the function as

```
crt_loca(position, c)          /* Not a good way to */
char c;                        /* define a function */
{
        . . .
}
```

The function will compile without error. However, in C, defining a function that relies on a default data type is sloppy. (The example relies on a default type-specifier int for the argument declaration of position.) Always be explicit in C to make debugging easier.

3.5. The most common mistake (especially by those who think they know it all?) is to reverse the positions of arguments in an argument list. For example, strcpy() is usually part of the standard library and is used to copy one string into another. The function states that the arguments are

```
strcpy(destination, source)
```

The function is designed to copy source into destination; that is, now there are two source strings. If you need a copy of name in dupli, it is very easy to call the function as

```
strcpy(name, dupli);           /* Wrong */
```

This statement copies the "garbage" in dupli right over the string you want. A related error is to forget to reserve enough space in dupli to place the null at the end of the dupli string.

If the arguments are reversed, the argument declarations may not be correct. For example, suppose that a function needs a char and an int as in

```
void func(letter, number)
char c;
int number;
{
        . . .
}
```

but in your program you call it as

```
func(x, alpha);
```

When you reverse the order, func() sees x as a char and alpha as an int. This can be a very subtle bug that may work *most* of the time. As you learn more about the other data types in C, the results of this kind of bug get interesting.

Finally, every C programmer has called a function with one argument when the function definition expects two. Often, you get a few undefined bytes of data popped off the stack when the function executes. What actually happens from that point on is unknown, but this condition is often an invitation for your program to go west (and lock up the computer).

3.6. There is really no difference. Some programmers, however, prefer to think of function arguments as existing only in the function definition. When the function is called, the variables passed to the function as part of the call are parameters, as in the following:

```
main()
{
    int x, y;
    . . .
    func(x, y);
    . . .
}

void func(a, b)
int a, b;
{
    . . .
}
```

Variables x and y are parameters (values) that are passed to func(), but arguments a and b assume meaningful values only after the function has been called. The view, therefore, is that parameters are values passed to the function and that arguments in a function definition have no useful values until after the parameters "reach" the function.

The distinction is minor unless it hinders communication with other C programmers.

3.7. Every variable in a C program has one of the following storage classes: external, static, automatic, or register. The *storage class* refers to the way the compiler allocates memory for a variable and function.

While you are reading the discussion that follows, keep in mind that variables in C must be defined in one of two places: outside or inside a function or statement block.

A variable that is defined outside a function block is said to have *external storage class*. The variable is available to whatever function needs it. Because functions cannot be defined within a function, all functions default to the external storage class. Figure 3.10 of the *Guide* uses variable x as an example of the external storage class. This is the default storage class for all variables defined outside a function block.

The keyword extern is used in a declaration when a variable with external storage class is defined somewhere else but must be used with the current function or file. Typically, the extern variable has been defined in a different file. Figure 3.11 in the *Guide* shows an example. In that figure, x is defined outside any function block in File 2. Therefore, x has external storage class. However, you want to use x in File 1 within a function block—that is, inside main() in File 1. Therefore, you must use the keyword extern to indicate that x is a variable with external storage class, but the variable is not defined in this file.

To drive the point home, consider what the compiler would do in the following situation:

```
File 1                    File 2

int x;

main()                    void func()
{                         {

    x = x + 1;                x = x + 2;
}                         }
```

When you compile File 1, there are no problems. Even though x is not defined within main(), the function knows all about x because x is defined outside a function block and is available to any function in File 1 that needs it.

Now try to compile File 2. You will get a "variable undefined" error message because the compiler does not know what data type x is. How do you solve the problem? By giving File 2 the needed information about x. You fix the problem by changing File 2 to be

```
File 2

extern int x;

void func()
{
    x = x + 2;
}
```

extern tells the compiler that x is defined somewhere else. In this case, x is defined in the first file. The int tells the compiler the data type and instructs the compiler to treat this variable as an integer. The x is simply the name, or identifier, of the variable and enables the compiler to find the variable when the two files are linked.

Note that after the two files are linked, x is available everywhere in the two files. That is, if func() is called after x is assigned a value of 1 in main(), the function call to func() changes x to 3 wherever else x may be used.

Variables defined outside a function block (external storage class) are initialized to zero when the program is executed. Therefore, x equals 1 in File 1 as it stands but equals 3 if func() is subsequently called.

The *static storage class* has two meanings: external and internal. A variable that has an external static storage class is available to any function that needs it, *but only within the file in which it is defined.* For example, consider the following files.

```
File 1                          File 2

int x;                          static int x;

main()                          void func()
{                               {

      x = x + 1;                      x = x + 2;
}                               }
```

Note how File 2 uses the keyword static in the definition of x. This usage means that x is available to any function that needs it in File 2, but *only* in File 2. Therefore, the *scope* of a static variable defined outside a function block is limited to the file in which the variable is defined.

The usage of the static definition also indicates that when files are linked, the compiler treats differently variables that have the same name but are in different files. File 1 and File 2 each have an x, but the compiler regards the x's as two different variables because of the static definition in File 2.

The external static storage class is a real asset because it allows you to create external storage class variables in one file without having to worry about "collisions" with variables of the same name in another file.

An internal static storage class refers to variables that are defined within a function block with the keyword static. Because internal static variables are defined within a function block, their scope is limited to the function block in which they are defined. An example follows.

```
int func(a)
int a;
{
    static int x = 1;
    x = a * x;
    return(x);
}
```

Suppose that you make a call to func() and that the value of a on this first call is 2. Because x is initialized to 1, the next line assigns the value 2 to x. Now suppose that you call func() a second time, with the value of a unchanged. Unlike the default storage class for variables defined within a function block (see the automatic storage class), an internal static variable retains its value between function calls. Therefore, on the second call to func(), the return value for x is 4 even though the value of the argument a is the same.

The keyword static used within a function block gives you a way of preserving the *previous* value of the variable. Internal static variables are initialized once (to zero by default) when the program is first run. Because internal static variables are not reinitialized every time the function is called, they retain their values between function calls.

Because memory is allocated for statics at compile time, they give two other benefits. First, static arrays can be initialized. (Auto storage class arrays cannot. Initializers will be discussed later.) Second, because the addresses of static arrays are known at run time, their addresses are not referenced off the stack, which can lead to a slight decrease in execution time. On the negative side, however, statics should not be used in recursive functions. Inasmuch as statics are not initialized with each invocation of the function and most recursive functions are based on a "fresh" set of variables, most recursive functions cannot use static variables.

The storage class for variables defined within a function is the *automatic storage class* and can be defined with the optional keyword auto. The scope of an automatic variable is limited to the function block in which it is defined. No other function has access to automatic storage class variables. They come to life when the function is entered, live privately within the function, and then "die" without a trace when control exits from the function.

Automatic storage class variables cannot retain their values between function calls. However, it is possible to initialize automatic storage class variables, but not arrays or structures. Each time the function block is called, a new set of automatic storage class variables is created. If initializers are present for any automatic storage class variable that is not an array or structure, the automatic variable is assigned this value each time the function is called.

The *register storage class* attempts to allocate a variable to a CPU (Central Processing Unit) register. Because most CPUs have a limited number of registers, there is no guarantee that the variable will be stored successfully in a register. If a CPU register is not available, the variable assumes the default automatic storage class.

Because CPU registers are of limited size, only certain data types (for example, char and int) fit in a register. Seeking the register storage class for an array of ints will not be successful and may return an error message.

In most respects, the register storage class behaves similarly to the automatic storage class. (No initializers are allowed, and the scope is limited to the function block in which the variable is defined.) The advantage is that register storage class variables are faster than automatic variables because the former reside within the CPU register and do not have to be fetched from memory and moved to a register for processing.

Storage class will be discussed further in later examples.

3.8. The storage class of a variable affects the way the variable is referenced when the program executes. (The register storage class is self-evident, so it will not be considered here.) For purposes of discussion, consider the default automatic storage class as compared to the external storage class. (The static storage class behaves in a manner that is similar to external variables in terms of address calculations.)

When the program is compiled, variables of the external storage class are allocated the required number of bytes to store whatever data type has been declared (for example, 2 or 4 bytes for an int). When the linker finishes its job, each variable has a fixed, known address. It is important that you realize that a variable's address is known before run time (when the user runs the program).

On the other hand, variables of the automatic storage class are most often referenced in relation to some other known point in the program (for instance, the stack). Offsets are calculated relative to the known point to locate the variable you actually want to use. This process takes time and code.

Therefore, everything else being equal, external variables usually execute faster than automatic variables. The next question gives some indication of how performance is affected.

3.9. Most working variables are defined within `main()` and therefore are of the automatic storage class. When I ran the program on my system (Z80 with a 4 MHz clock speed and no wait states), the program took 29.35 seconds.

Now to play devil's advocate: If external storage class variables are more efficient, you should be able to see some improvement in speed by moving the variables outside `main()`. The first change is to move

```
int i, prime, k, count, iter;
```

so that it appears outside `main()`. The first section might then look like

```
#define TRUE    1
#define FALSE   0
#define SIZE 8190

char    flags[SIZE+1];
int i, prime, k, count, iter;

main()
{
    . . .
```

I recompiled and ran the program. The time dropped to 20.03 seconds. Not bad—a 30 percent improvement.

You should also remember the discussion about CPU efficiency when comparing `int` and `unsigned` data types. Because most CPUs are designed to do unsigned arithmetic, check the code to see whether enough compares warrant the change. The first loop on `iter` does only 10 compares, so you shouldn't expect much here. However, inside the `iter` loop are three other `for` loops, each of which loops around SIZE times (8190). Some quick calculations suggest that here you may perform more than 160,000 compares. That number is large enough for you to make your external declarations the unsigned data type. Therefore try

```
#define TRUE   1
#define FALSE  0
#define SIZE 8190


char      flags[SIZE+1];

unsigned int i, prime, k, count, liter;
main()
{
      . . .
```

The new version of the program required 16.25 seconds for me.

Finally, note that the purpose of the first i loop is simply to place a value of 1 in the flags[] array. However, this loop is done 10 times, making 81,900 assignments. In some compilers' standard library is a function called setmem() that serves the same purpose. Because setmem() is usually written in assembler, the function may be faster at initializing the array.

By using setmem(), the program took only 13.11 seconds to execute.

Remember the old saying: "If it ain't broke, don't fix it." But like most old sayings, there's a flaw in its logic. By looking at the storage classes, recalling what your standard library contains and making a few quick changes, you can cut the execution time by almost 70 percent. Not all programs show this much improvement, but rethinking how the variables and their storage classes are used sometimes does pay off.

3.10. The answer to this question is obviously no. First, not all programs are based on algorithms that use this much looping. Therefore, making the variables external will not improve the program considerably. Second, and far more important, is the issue of privacy afforded automatic variables. Because their scope is the block in which they are defined (not of the external storage class and not available throughout the program), there is less chance of inadvertently changing their value. This kind of privacy becomes more and more important as program size increases.

Another consideration is whether the code is called recursively. That is, does the function call itself (direct recursion), or does the function call another function that calls this function (indirect recursion)? If the function is called recursively, automatic variables are probably needed so that the function will work properly.

As a general rule, use the external storage class only in cases where the variable is heavily used in many different functions throughout the program and where many functions need the current value of the variable to accomplish their tasks.

3.11. Yes. (I was really tempted to end the answer here!) Try changing the

```
main()
{
     int i, prime, k, count, iter;
     . . .
```

to

```
main()
{
     static unsigned int i, prime, k, count, iter;
     . . .
```

See what happens to the execution speed. Are the working variables available outside `main()`? How do you explain what happens? Is it necessary to make variables external to improve speed at the cost of privacy? (Review 3.8 for help.)

3.12. The purpose of an argument list in a function call is to send the *value* of the variable to any function that needs it. This feature allows a function to receive a *copy* of the variable for use outside the block in which the variable is defined.

It is critical that you understand that the called function is using not the actual variable but a copy of the variable. To prove this to yourself, type the following program and run it. (The & operator used in the program is not discussed until Chapter 4; call it the "address of" operator for the time being.)

```
include <stdio.h>

main()
{
        int i = 0;
        void func();
```

```
        printf("\nThe address of i is %u\n", &i);
        printf("and its value is %d n", i);

        func(i);

        printf("\nAfter the call to func() i = %d\n", i);
}

void func(i)
int i;
{
        printf("\nThe address of i in func() is\%u\n", &i);
        printf("and its value is %d\n", i);

        i = i + 5;

        printf("and its value in func() is now %d\n", i);
}
```

When you run the program, notice that the address of i in main() is *not* the same as the address of i in func(). The i in func() is a copy, or clone, of the i in main(). The two are not the same variable, as the different addresses for i prove.

Also note that the value of i in main() remains 0 even though the value was 5 in the final printf() in func(). The scope of an automatic variable is limited to the block in which it is defined; therefore, the i in main() cannot exist, or be seen, outside main().

The same is true for the i in func() because i is a temporary variable created only when func() is called. The scope of i is such that it dies when the program leaves func().

It should be clear that a function cannot alter the value of a variable that has the automatic or internal static storage class. (The only exceptions occur in arrays or when you use pointers to the variables. See 3.13 and Chapter 4.)

3.13. Arrays are an exception. Type the following program.

```
#include <stdio.h>

main()
{
        int i[10];
        void func();
```

```
        i[0] = 0;

        printf("\ni[0]'s value is %d\n", i[0]);

        func(i);

        printf("\nAfter the call to func(), i[0] = %d\n", i[0]);
}


void func(i)
int i[];
{
        printf("\nin func(), i[0]'s value is %d\n", i[0]);

        i[0] = i[0] + 5;

        printf("and its value is now %d\n", i[0]);
}
```

The initial value of element i[0] is 0. The program then calls func() by using the name of the array and prints the value of i[0] to show that it is still 0 inside func(). You then add 5 to i[0] and show that it is 5 while in func(). So far, everything is similar to the process in 3.12.

However, when i[0] is printed in main() after the call to func(), i[0] has a value of 5. This tells you that, for all intents and purposes, the original array is sent to a function when called. Unlike other automatic storage variables, arrays are not copied. If arrays were copied, func() could not have permanently altered the contents of i[0].

For the time being, simply remember that arrays are *not* copied when they are arguments in a function call. This subject is covered in greater detail in Chapter 4.

3.14. Perhaps the most fruitful area for program improvement is in the algorithm on which the program is built. An interesting example is found in an article by Jon Bentley in *Communications of the ACM*, 27, No. 9 (September, 1984), 865-869. The task was to process an array of numbers in a specific way. The first algorithm worked but took an increasingly longer time to process the array as the number of elements increased. Bentley's search for an improved algorithm produced three more algorithms (each of which worked, by the way) before he found one that produced reasonably quick results.

The article concludes with test results. Bentley's first algorithm was run on a Cray-1 (one of the fastest computers in the world). The fourth, and final, algorithm was run on a TRS-80 computer (not the fastest microcomputer around). For an array of 10,000 numbers, the first algorithm took 49 minutes to run on the Cray-1, whereas the same number of elements with the fourth algorithm on the TRS-80 required only 3.2 minutes. Extrapolating these results shows that if there were a million elements in the array, the first algorithm would take 95 *years* to run on a supercomputer, but the last algorithm would take only 5.4 *hours* on a small personal computer.

The message is clear: Just because the program works doesn't mean that it's efficient. A little additional thought about the algorithm can often produce dramatic improvements in the program.

3.15. The obvious way is to use the `extern` keyword for every variable in each supporting file. That's the hard way. Instead, you can create a header file that is read into each supporting file during the preprocessor pass. Call this header file `globals.h`. (The `.h` extension is commonly used for header files.) The `globals.h` header file might look as follows:

```
/*    This is the globals header file used in each support
module used with the program XXX0.C.
*/

      #if EXT
            extern
      #endif
                    char string[MAX];    /* Used for ...    */

      #if EXT
            extern
      #endif
                    int x;               /* Used for ...    */

      #if EXT
            extern
      #endif
                    ...                  /* And so on for   */
                    ...                  /* The rest of them */
```

In the example, the `#if` is a macro preprocessor directive that translates as follows: If the symbolic constant EXT is logical True (nonzero) in this file, place the word `extern` in the file at this point.

The #endif marks the end of the #if conditional preprocessor directive.

Now suppose that file0 is the main() module and files file1 through file5 are the support modules. Begin file1 through file5 with:

```
#define EXT 1          /* Extern declarations needed */
#include "globals.h"   /* File with the globals    */
   ...
```

The #include directive causes the globals.h file to be read into the program at this point. Note that this is a source code file; it is not compiled separately.

Because the #define EXT 1 would appear first in files file1 through file5, the symbolic constant EXT is defined as True for file. When the header file is read in, the #if statements are logic True, so the keyword extern appears before each declaration. After the preprocessor pass is completed, the declarations in files file1 through file5 appear as

```
extern char string[MAX];  /* Used for ...    */
extern int x;             /* Used for ...    */
extern    ...             /* And so on for   */
   ...                    /* The rest of them */
```

This is exactly what you need.

You still have a problem, however. The main() module cannot contain the keyword extern because the variables must be defined in the main() module. (If all files used extern, the compiler could never find the actual definitions.) The solution is simple. The first thing in file0 that contains main() is

```
#define EXT 0           /* No Extern declarations */
#include "globals.h"    /* File with the globals */
   ...
main()
{
   ...                  /* Rest of program      */
   ...
```

Because EXT is now defined in main() as logical False, the keyword extern is not placed in this file by the preprocessor. The definitions will appear as needed in file 0.

```
char string[MAX];    /* Used for ...     */
int x;               /* Used for ...     */
    ...              /* And so on for    */
    ...              /* The rest of them */
```

The major advantage is that you have to type the file globals.h only once, thus reducing the chance of error, because you are not retyping the lists of variables in every supporting file. Adding or deleting global variables is also much easier because you edit only one file. You do not have to change any other source file.

This method can be a real time-saver.

3.16. There are many ways to write the function, one of which is

```
#include <stdio.h>

main()
{
        int base, j;
        char s[20];
        char *gets();
        void cvt();

        printf("Enter a number base: ");
        base = atoi(gets(s));
        printf("\n\nEnter a number: ");
        j = atoi(gets(s));

        cvt(j, base);
}

/*****
     Function to convert base 10 number to another base
     within the range of base 2 through base 16. The function
     displays the conversion as part of the function.

     Argument list: int value      the value to convert
                    int base        the base used

     Return value: nothing useful returned from function
*****/

void cvt(value, base)
int value, base;
{
        int i = 0;
        static char vals[] = "0123456789abcdef";
        char c[20];
```

```
do {
        c[i++] = vals[value % base];
} while ((value /= base) != 0);

while (i--)
        putchar(c[i]);
}
```

Note how the vals[] character array is initialized inside the function. You can initialize internal static arrays, but automatic arrays cannot be initialized. The contents of the vals[] array is used to fill the c[] character array for printing. If you study the way the algorithm works, you will notice that the c[] array is filled in "backward" from the way it must be printed. The while(i--) prints the converted number as you would expect to see it.

If you do not want to print the converted number as part of the function, you can pass an array to the function as part of the argument list and use that array instead of c[].

As a related exercise, write a new function that copies the contents of the c[] into another array in the "forward" direction. (That is, copy c[] into x[] in a way that allows you to print x[] as a normal string.)

3.17. When I first started programming, someone told me that 70 percent of the time required to develop a program was spent designing the program. I didn't believe it then, and I don't believe it now. It's more like 80 to 90 percent. Design efforts can pay off handsomely in C.

C lends itself nicely to modular design. After the task of the program has been specified, the next question is how to do it. Most programming problems can be broken down into at least five smaller steps:

> initialization
> input
> processing
> output
> termination

These five steps can be applied to something as large as a complete program or as small as a single function.

Initialization usually involves declaring variables and establishing symbolic constants for the preprocessor. The input step requires getting the necessary data into the program. This information might come from the user through the keyboard or from a disk data file. The processing step involves reorganizing the data in a way that solves the task at hand. The output step requires presenting the data in a usable form. The output might go to the CRT, printer, or disk data file. The termination step is a "clean up" that may or may not be necessary, depending on how the previous four steps were used. For example, if disk data files were used, they need to be closed. Perhaps this section of the program holds intermediate results that must be passed on to another section of the program. Very simple programs may just return to the operating system after termination.

Once a program has been outlined using the steps suggested, the details of each step can be designed. The details represent a "sideways" movement, and program flow is "top-down." This is illustrated in the following chart:

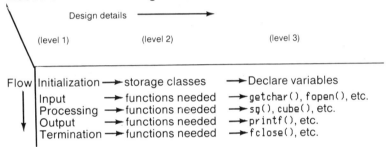

In all but the smallest programs, a table patterned after (and expanded from) this one is a first step in designing a program. This approach identifies the functions needed (including any new ones that must be created) before a single line of code is written. The fourth level of design detail is the algorithm used to write the new function, and level 5 is the actual code itself.

Try this approach on a simple program and see whether the method doesn't help crystalize things in your mind.

3.18. Symbolic constants are easy to change when necessary, but this method has two drawbacks. First, you must go into each source file and edit the #defines. On large projects this can be a time-consuming task. Second, after the symbolic constants have been edited, you must recompile, assemble, and link all the files in which the constants were used. Normally, this task takes more time than editing the files.

A better approach is to write a function that contains the code necessary to accomplish whatever the #define was designed to do. For example,

```
void clrscr()
{

      printf("%s", "\033*");

}
```

replaces

```
#define CLEAR  "\033*"
...
printf(CLEAR);
```

Both approaches clear the screen (assuming the codes are correct for the terminal at hand).

The advantage of using a function, however, is that you need only to recompile the library module that contains the new clrscr() function and then relink the programs. By making the task a function call and placing it in a library module, you avoid recompiling and assembling each C source program. If time is allocated equally among compile, assembly, and link times, you have just reduced your revision time by two-thirds.

Keep this in mind when you consider using symbolic constants for hardware-dependent tasks.

4
Pointers

Questions about Pointers

4.1. In one sentence, state what a pointer is. *(Answer on p. 76.)*

4.2. What is the form of a pointer definition in a program? *(Answer on p. 76.)*

4.3. How much storage does a pointer require? Does it vary according to the type of data to which it points? *(Answer on p. 77.)*

4.4. My compiler documentation says that the compiler supports "both large and small models." What does this mean? *(Answer on p. 78.)*

4.5. What are lvalues and rvalues? *(Answer on p. 79.)*

4.6. In Chapter 3, I explained that arguments in a function call pass to a function *copies* of variables, not the actual variables. Therefore, the function cannot directly alter the value of the variable. How can you pass a variable to a function so that the function permanently changes the value of that variable? Write a function that permanently changes a number in a different function to a positive value if the number is negative. *(Answer on p. 82.)*

4.7. As mentioned in Chapter 3, array variables are not copied when passed to a function. How does this fact relate to the current discussion of pointers? *(Answer on p. 84.)*

4.8. Write a function that, on finding a specified character (c) in a string, returns the rest of the string. For example, if the string is "Indianapolis, IN 46220", look for a comma and return the address of the remainder of the string. *(Answer on p. 86.)*

4.9. If ptr is a "pointer to int" that has been properly initialized to point to an array of integers and j is an integer, what does the following statement do? *(Answer on p. 89.)*

```
j = *(ptr + 1);
```

4.10. Most C programmers would not write the program the way it was presented in 4.9. What changes do you think an experienced programmer would make? *(Answer on p. 90.)*

4.11. Chapter 3 contains a program that converts a decimal number to the same number for any base up to 16. Given what you've learned so far, will the following version of the function work? Why or why not? *(Answer on p. 91.)*

```
void cvt(value, base)
int value, base;
{
        int i = 0;
        char c[20];

        do {
                c[i++] = "0123456789abcdef"[value % base];
        } while ((value /= base) != 0);

        while (i--)
                putchar(c[i]);
}
```

4.12. Assume that you are designing a program you expect to sell worldwide. You want the program translated into other languages, but you don't want anyone else to see the source code. (You've done some very clever things in the program.) How would you solve both the translation and the protection problems? *(Answer on p. 91.)*

4.13. Write a program with which you can enter a memory address and the number of addresses to be displayed starting with the address entered. Display the addresses and their contents in hexadecimal. (A nice touch would be to display the contents in ASCII, too.) *(Answer on p. 94.)*

4.14. The program discussed in 4.13 works fine, but if a large number of addresses are to be displayed, the information scrolls across the screen faster than you can read it. Add a pause() function that stops the display when the screen is full. *(Answer on p. 97.)*

4.15. Write a sample program that contains a "pointer to function." Why may such a data construct be useful? *(Answer on p. 99.)*

4.16. What is the difference between the following declarations? *(Answer on p. 101.)*

```
void func1(s)              void func2(s)
char s[];                  char *s;
{                          {
      . . .                      . . .
}                          }
```

Answers to Questions about Pointers

4.1. A pointer is a variable that contains the address of another variable.

Although the definition of a pointer is simple, using pointers is difficult for the beginning C programmer. Several questions in this chapter are devoted to the trouble spots that most beginners have difficulty understanding. I encourage you to stick with pointers until "the penny drops." If you are like most programmers just getting started with pointers, the concepts will seem obscure for a while. Then, suddenly, everything will fall into place.

4.2. The general form for a pointer definition is

```
data type      *identifier;
   (3)          (1)   (2)
```

The compiler needs to know three pieces of information about a pointer. First, the compiler needs to know that the variable will be used as a pointer. The asterisk (∗) in the definition tells the compiler that you are defining a pointer variable. Whenever you define a pointer variable, the asterisk must appear in the definition.

Second, the compiler needs the name of the variable that will be used as a pointer. Obviously, the compiler must create a label for this variable. The usual naming rules apply to pointers.

Third, the compiler *must* have the type of data being pointed to by this variable. This information is critical because every pointer has a *scalar* value or size associated with it. The scalar size is the number of bytes required to store the data type to which the pointer is pointing. If you define a pointer to a character

```
char *letter;
```

the definition of the pointer variable letter typically has a scalar size of one. If you declare a pointer to an integer

```
int *number;
```

the definition of number has a scalar size of two for 8- and 16-bit computers and a scalar size of four for 32-bit computers. The actual size of the scalar depends on the computer being used. A summary of typical scalar sizes follows:

Data Type	Scalar Size	
	8- and 16-bit computers	*32-bit computers*
char	1	1
int	2	4
short	2	2
long	4	4
float	4	4
double	8	8

Other data types will be discussed later.

The compiler must be given the data type, and hence the scalar size because you frequently need to increment or decrement a pointer. The scalar size tells the compiler how many bytes to use in the increment or decrement operation. For example, if you have a pointer that points to an array of integers and you increment the pointer by one, the compiler uses the scalar size to determine where the next integer in the array is located. Therefore, when your program increments the pointer by one, the compiler must actually skip 2 bytes (or 4 on a 32-bit computer) to find the next integer in the array. If you increment a pointer by one to a double, the compiler must skip over 8 bytes to find the next double.

Fortunately, the compiler uses the scalar automatically; you don't have to worry about it. However, think of the problems caused when you define a pointer to a character and then set the pointer to the address of an array of integers. If you increment the pointer by one, the compiler has been told in the declaration that its scalar is one, but you are using the pointer as though its scalar were two (or four). A common mistake made by beginning C programmers is to declare the pointer one way and use it in an entirely different way. You're assuming one value for the scalar, and the compiler is using another. Pointers rarely work this way.

4.3. The size of a pointer is equal to the amount of storage needed to hold a memory address of the host computer. Because pointers hold *only* the address of some other variable, all pointers are usually the same size regardless of the data type to which they point.

Most 8- and 16-bit microcomputers take 2 bytes to store a memory address. 32-bit computers take 4 bytes to store a memory address. Therefore, every pointer in an 8- or 16-bit system requires 2 bytes, and every pointer in a 32-bit system requires 4 bytes whether the pointer has been defined to point to a character, a `double`, or any other data type.

However, certain "fuzzy areas" exist for pointer storage, as treated in the next question.

4.4. In the "old days," microcomputers were limited in the amount of memory they could address (64 kilobytes, or 64K) because the Central Processing Unit (CPU) had only 16 address lines available. Only 2 states can exist on an address line (on or off), so the maximum amount of memory available was 65,536 bytes (2 raised to the 16th power). Popular CPUs using such addressing include the Z80, 8080, 6502, and 6800.

It wasn't long before people started getting cranky about the memory limitations of these chips. As a result, CPU chip manufacturers added another register (often called a segment register) that allowed multiple "banks" of 64K to be used. As a result, these new chips can address millions of bytes of memory even though the CPUs still use only 16 address lines. The Intel 8086 family, which includes the 8088 and 80186, is a common example of "segmented" CPUs.

These differences affect the way pointers are stored in the computer. A compiler that uses the "small model" normally uses 2 bytes (16 bits) for storing a pointer. As a result, the maximum program size is 128K (64K for program code and 64K for program data).

A compiler that uses the "large model" normally uses 4 bytes (32 bits) for storing a pointer. As a result, significantly larger amounts of memory (megabytes) can be addressed by a pointer, and programs can be much larger. The price of using this increased memory is increased time to manipulate pointers because twice as much data for each pointer must be processed.

Which model should you use if both are available? If you are just learning C, use the small model. Because processing time (compile, assembly, and link times) is less for the small model, it should give a slightly faster "turn around" time, which can be important while you are learning C. A complete set of exception rules to C exists for large model programs. For these reasons, learn C, using the small model.

If you are using a computer with a Motorola 68000, National Semiconductor 32000, or Digital Equipment VAX CPU, you are using the equivalent of a "large model" compiler on CPUs that are "nonsegmented." The compiler on your systems can address megabytes of memory and does not have the exception rules as do compilers for the Intel 8086 family.

For large projects under the 8086 family, however, you may have to learn the exception rules and use the large model. I suggest that you stick to the small model until you have learned the language; then graduate to "large model" programming.

4.5. Every variable has some unique place in memory where the variable is stored by the compiler. This address is the variable's lvalue. In reality, the working program never uses the name you give a variable in your program; the program uses only the variable's lvalue, or address.

To be useful in a program, every variable must also contain a piece of information. This data is the variable's rvalue, the contents of the variable.

Therefore, the lvalue tells the compiler where to go in memory to find the variable, and the rvalue is the contents of that variable. It seems obvious, then, that you need to have one operator for the address of a variable (lvalue) and a different operator for the contents of a variable (rvalue).

To illustrate, create an integer variable named x and then assign the value of 5 to it. The code fragment to do this might be

```
int x;

x = 5;
```

Further assume that the compiler stores the variable x at memory location 60,000. The relationship is diagrammed below.

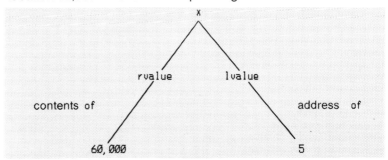

The lvalue uses the ampersand (&) to determine the address of a variable, and the rvalue of a variable uses the asterisk (*) to get the contents of the variable. (Note: The "contents of" operator [*] can be used properly only with a variable that has been defined as a pointer variable.)

At this point some things may seem confusing because the asterisk is used in two different ways. First, the asterisk is used in a definition to indicate that a pointer variable is being created; and second, the asterisk is used to determine the *rvalue* of a variable. How do you know which is which?

Refer to the discussion in 4.2. The purpose of the asterisk in a definition like

```
char *letter;
```

is to tell the compiler that you want to use letter as a pointer variable, which is to be scaled to the size of a character if and when you manipulate it.

What does letter point to below?

```
main()
{
     char *letter;
}
```

Who knows! The sole purpose of a pointer is to hold a memory address of another variable. The compiler will create a place in memory for letter, but it's anybody's guess as to what address is contained at letter's memory location. Nothing useful is contained in letter until you give it something to point to.

Now consider

```
main()
{
        char *letter;        /* Line 1 */
        char c;              /* Line 2 */

        c = 'A';             /* Line 3 */

        letter = &c;         /* Line 4 */
}
```

A character variable c (line 2) has been created, and the letter A assigned to it (line 3).

Now examine closely what line 4 does. It translates: Take the address of c (its *lvalue* because of the & operator) and assign it to letter. Because you have defined letter to be a pointer, it is designed to hold an address; and in line 4, the program assigns the address of c to letter.

If the compiler creates the variable letter at memory location 59,000 and variable c at location 60,000, the following table summarizes the control flow of the program.

Line No.	Variable	lvalue	rvalue
1	letter	59,000	(junk)
2	c	60,000	(junk)
3	c	60,000	A
4	letter	59,000	60,000

The table demonstrates that line 1 creates letter at memory location 59,000 (*lvalue*), and it contains whatever junk happens to be there when it is created. (Only external and static storage class variables are initialized to zero.)

Line 2 creates c at memory location 60,000, which also contains junk at this point. Line 3 assigns the character A to c. If you look at memory location 60,000 (*lvalue*), you will find an A there (*rvalue*).

Line 4 does the neat stuff. It takes the address of c (its *lvalue* of 60,000) and assigns *that address* to letter. The content of letter (its *rvalue*) is now 60,000. You have initialized letter to point to something useful, the variable c.

Now print the contents of letter, using the asterisk ("contents of") operator.

```
#include <stdio.h>

main()
{
        char *letter;          /* Line 1 */
        char c;                /* Line 2 */

        c = 'A';               /* Line 3 */

        letter = &c;           /* Line 4 */

        printf("The contents of letter = %c\n", *letter);
}
```

Note how the printf() is used. You defined letter a "pointer to char," so you use the %c conversion character in printf() because the pointer is scaled for a character.

When the compiler senses *letter in printf(), the program responds, "Because I know that letter is a pointer, I'll go to letter at its *lvalue* of 59,000 and, because pointers hold memory addresses, get the address stored there (letter's *rvalue* of 60,000) and print whatever is stored *at location 60,000* as a character." Note that the "contents of" operator (*) does *not* cause the printing of the *rvalue* of the pointer variable but rather the contents of the address of what is stored in the pointer. This process of indirection makes the behavior of pointers different from that of any other type of variable in C.

I urge you to diagram the preceding discussion so that you can visualize what is actually going on in a short program. If you want to see what the numbers look like, try the following program.

```
#include <stdio.h>

main()
{
        char *letter;           /* Line 1 */
        char c;                 /* Line 2 */

        c = 'A';                /* Line 3 */

        letter = &c;            /* Line 4 */

        printf("The contents of letter = %c\n", *letter);
        printf("lvalue of letter = %u\n", &letter);
        printf("rvalue of letter = %u\n", letter);
        printf("lvalue of c = %u\n", &c);
        printf("rvalue of c = %c\n", c);

}
```

Why must you use the %u conversion character in the printf()s? Because memory addresses will likely exceed the range of an integer variable, and memory addresses are never negative.

Experiment with these ideas until pointers are clear to you.

4.6. Obviously, you need to use a pointer in the function and pass the address of the variable to be changed. One solution to the question might be as follows:

```
#include <stdio.h>

main()
{
```

```
        int i;
        char buff[10];
        char *gets();
        void absolute();

        printf("Enter a number: ");

        i = atoi(gets(buff));

        absolute(&i);                /* Note we're sending the */
                                     /* address of i here      */

        printf("\n\nThe value is %d\n", i);
}
/*****
        Function takes integer x and changes
        it to a positive number if negative

        Argument list: int *x      number to change if negative

        Return value: none

        CAUTION:       number is permanently changed if negative
*****/

void absolute(x)
int *x;                         /* Because it's declared as a    */
{                               /* pointer, it gets an address   */

        if (*x < 0)             /* Must use "contents of" to get */
            *x = -*x;           /* the value of i                */

}                               /* No return value needed because*/
                                /* changed original variable     */
```

The first part of main() should be familiar to you by now. When you call absolute(), the argument being passed is the address of variable i. You can use the "address of" operator (&) with any variable.

Once you enter absolute(), you know that x contains the address of variable i in main(). Because you have declared x to be a pointer, the compiler expects it to contain an address (which it does). Although x contains an address, the compiler needs the value of what is *stored* at that address; therefore, the rest of the references to x must use the "contents of" operator (*) for the function to work properly.

The remainder of the function changes the sign of the variable if it is less than zero. Because you can change the value of i in main() in the function, you do not need to have a return value in the function.

To gain some familiarity with your compiler, change the declaration of x in absolute() to a plain integer declaration (no pointer) and see what happens. You should get an error message stating that an illegal indirection is in the line containing the if statement. (That is, you used an int as a pointer when it wasn't declared to be a pointer.) This message reinforces the fact that you cannot use the "contents of" operator (*) unless it is used with a variable that has been declared a pointer.

4.7. As you recall, when arrays are used as arguments in a function call, the address of element 0 of the array is passed to the function. Can you prove this fact in the following program?

```
#include <stdio.h>

main()
{

        void func();

        static char s[] = {'a', 'b', 'c', 'd', '\0'};

        printf("In main(), address of s[0] = %u\n", &s[0]);
        func(s);
}

/*****
        Function prints out the contents of an array of
        characters

        Argument list: char s[]    an array of characters

        Return value: none
*****/

void func(c)
char c[];
{
        printf("%s", c);
        printf("\nIn func(), the address of c[0] = %u\n", &c[0]);
}
```

In main(), variable s[] is declared a static array of characters. The static storage class enables you to initialize the character array with several letters followed by a null character, which makes it possible for you to print the character array as a string. You then print the address of where the character array resides in memory.

The program next calls func(), which prints the contents of the array and then the address of the first element in the string. You will note that both addresses are the same even though one is in main() and the other is in func(). Therefore, you know that the address of s[] has been passed to func() because s[] is an array.

Interesting! If the address of an array is passed, you should be able to use what is passed to func() as though it were a pointer. Edit the program to reflect the new declaration for s[] in main() and c in func().

```
#include <stdio.h>

main()
{
        void func();

        static char s[] = "abcd";     /* Initialized as string */

        printf("In main(), address of s[0] = %u\n", &s[0]);
        func(s);
}

/*****
        Function prints out the contents of an array of
        characters

        Argument list: s[]    an array of characters

        Return value: none
*****/

void func(c)
char *c;                              /* Now viewed as a pointer */
{
        printf("%s\n", c);
        printf("\nIn func(), the address of c[0] = %u\n", &c[0]);
}
```

There are two further interesting facts about these changes. First, you can initialize an internal static array with a string constant. The compiler automatically appends the null character (\Ø) to the end of the string constant. Second, you can declare c in func() to be a pointer, without altering the way the program works.

This discussion shows several things. First, on function calls, arrays are not copied; the address of the first element in the array is passed to the function. The way you called func() in main() also shows that using s and using &s[Ø] are the same. The name of the array and its first element yield the same address. (Skeptics can change the function call to func(&s[Ø]) to prove this if they wish.)

The second and third points concern declaring the array in the receiving function. The second point is that if an array is passed to a function, you can declare the array to be an array (char c[]) or a pointer (char *c). This option has important implications because pointers are processed faster in certain circumstances.

Third, if you declare the array to be an array, you do not have to supply an element value in the declaration. That is, you do not need to say char c[5]; you can use just char c[]. You do not need to declare an element value, because, to the compiler, the array is just an address; you aren't copying the array itself. The compiler works on the assumption that you won't try to get more elements out of the array than you defined.

Keep in mind that if you declare a variable

```
char s[1Ø];
```

a statement like

```
c = s[1Ø];
```

is incorrect even though the compiler does accept it. You have only 10 elements in s[], so valid boundaries are s[Ø] through s[9], not s[1Ø]. To C, zero is a real counting number, and all arrays start with element 0. (You'll remember this better if you make this mistake and the system goes to never-never land.)

Experiment with the suggested variations to prove to yourself that these conclusions are correct.

4.8. This could be written many ways.

```
#include <stdio.h>

main()
{
```

```
          static char s[] = "Indianapolis, IN 46220";
          char *ser_ret();
          char *new;

          new = ser_ret(s, ',' );
          if(new != NULL)
                  printf("\nThe return string is %s\n", new);
          else
                  printf("\nThe character was not found\n");
}

char *ser_ret(str, c)
char *str;                      /* The string to search    */
char c;                         /* The character to look for */
{

          while (*str != c && *str != '\0' )
                  ++str;
          if (*str == '\0' )
                  return (NULL);
          else
                  return (++str);  /* Increment past comma    */
}
```

I chose to start with an initialized static character array, but you might accept the input of the string and the character from the keyboard.

The program then calls ser_ret() with the address of the string to search and the character used in the search. Declare the address of the string to be a pointer. The while loop looks through the string to see that it is not equal to c or a null character (end-of-string). If these conditions are met, the pointer is incremented.

Note the importance of the scalar used by str in the increment operation. Because str is a "pointer to char," the scalar is one byte, which marches you through the character array by the correct size each time the increment operation (++) is performed.

The while loop terminates on reaching one of two conditions: c matches an element of the s[] array, or the null character in s[] is encountered. The pointer now points at either the character for which you are looking (the comma) or the null.

An if test checks whether the pointer str points to the null character. If so, c (the comma) was not found in the array passed from main(). Here, we return NULL from the function. We'll explain NULL later in this answer.

If c is found in s[], the else statement is executed. str now points to the search character. The pointer must be incremented one more time to get past the comma. This is a preincrement operator (the ++ being in front of the variable name); the pointer is incremented before the program returns the address of the pointer to main().

Back in main(), the program assigns to new the address returned from ser_ret(). Because new is a character pointer, it is properly declared to receive an address. An if-else test checks whether new is not equal to NULL. If new does not equal NULL, the program then simply prints the rest of the string, starting with the address of the first character appearing after the comma in the string. If new is a null pointer, an error message is printed.

Note the several pieces of defensive coding. You declared ser_ret() as

```
char *ser_ret(str, c);
```

Why do you use char * before the function name? You are returning a "pointer to char" from the function. You know this from the argument declarations in ser_ret(). You declared str to be a "pointer to char," and str is being returned from the function.

You will recall that the default data type returned from a function call is int. Because pointers and ints are different in C (even though they may take the same amount of storage), place the exact data type returned from the function in front of the function name when the function is defined.

The second piece of defensive coding is to declare what the function returns in main(). If you do not, the compiler will "think" the function is returning an integer from ser_ret() rather than a "pointer to char." In a real sense, this is not defensive coding but a necessity for the program to work properly.

Depending on the compiler, the program may or may not work without these precautions. However, it is always a good idea to declare exactly what is being returned from the function. If whatever is being returned from a function is not an integer data type, the function should also be declared in the function block that called it—for example, main().

The program uses NULL in two places. What is NULL? NULL is a symbolic value typically #defined in the stdio.h header file to be the value of 0. In C, a pointer that has been assigned the integer value of zero is guaranteed not to point at any object. This pointer, called a *null pointer*, will never point at any valid information.

By using `return (NULL);`, we are actually returning a null pointer to `main()` from `ser_ret()`. For functions that return a pointer, the common technique is to return a null pointer if the activity in the function failed. In the case of `ser_ret()`, returning NULL signifies that the search character was not found in the array of `chars`.

The `if-else` test in `main()` checks whether a valid pointer was returned from `ser_ret()`. If `new` is a non-null pointer (`!= NULL`), `ser_ret()` found the search character, and we print the remainder of the string. If `new` is a null pointer, we print the error message instead.

As this program is written, we will never see the error message. To see the error message, change the line

```
new = ser_ret(s, ',');
```

to

```
new = ser_ret(s, 'b');
```

then recompile and rerun the program.

4.9. Because the pointer has been initialized, it points to the first element in the array of integers. That is, the rvalue of `ptr` is the address of element 0 of the array. Assume that the array is named `i[]` and is located at memory location 55,000. Therefore, the rvalue of `ptr` is 55,000, the location of `i[0]`.

The statement adds 1 to `ptr` because the hierarchy of operators forces the operations in parentheses to be evaluated first. What is the rvalue of `ptr` at this time? It is *not* 55,001, because `ptr` is a "pointer to `int`," which has a scalar of 2. The rvalue of `ptr` is now 55,002. You know now that `ptr` is pointing to the second element of the integer array (`i[1]`).

The expression in parentheses has been evaluated, so the "contents of" operator tells you to get the value stored at memory location 55,002 and assign it to `j`. The line increments the pointer and takes the (assumed-to-be) integer value there and assigns it to `j`.

The following program illustrates these concepts.

```
#include <stdio.h>

main()
{
        int i[10], *ptr, j;

        j = 0;
        while (j < 10)
                i[j] = j++;     /* Fill the array with 0-9     */

        ptr = i;                /* Initialize the pointer to i */
        j = 0;
                                /* Now print the array         */
        while (j < 10) {
                printf("\ni[%d] = %d", j, *(ptr + j));
                ++j;
        }
}
```

The program is straightforward and needs no explanation. The only unusual part is the last argument in printf(), the subject of this question.

The important thing to remember is that (assuming the pointer has been initialized to point to i)

    j = *(ptr + 1);

is the same as

    j = i[1];

Either form accomplishes the same thing. Does it matter which one is used? Maybe. Most compilers are slightly more efficient manipulating pointers than they are calculating array indexes. Given a choice, use pointers instead of array indexes.

4.10. The program presented in 4.9 was created to illustrate a point. In "the real world," the same program would probably be written as follows:

```
#include <stdio.h>

main()
{
        int i[10], *ptr, j = 0;

        while (j < 10)
                i[j] = j++;
```

```
    ptr = i;

    j = 0;

    while (j < 10)
        printf("\ni[%d] = %d", j++, *ptr++);
}
```

In this example, the *ptr++ uses operators that have the same hierarchy. However, because you are using a postincrement on the pointer, the contents of the pointer are used (printed) before the pointer is incremented. The rest of the program is much the same as the one in 4.9.

4.11. This function works the same as the earlier version. Indeed, only the statement controlled by the do-while appears a little strange because the string constant (the characters enclosed by double quotation marks) is followed by what appears to be an array index. The program seems to be using an array that has no name. How can it work?

First, in the "eyes" of the compiler, a string constant resolves to an array of characters. As such, the compiler will always treat the string constant as "pointer to char." As you learned in 4.9, you can also treat array indexes and pointers the same way.

If you pretend that the compiler created and initialized a pointer to the string constant with the name c_ptr, the statement

```
    c[i++] = "0123456789abcdef"[value % base];
```

appears to the compiler as

```
    c[i++] = c_ptr[value % base];
```

This logic also extends to your standard library. For example, the string concatenation function is written with two arguments that have argument declarations of "pointer to char." You can also call the string concatenation function

```
    strcat("Indianapolis    ", ", ", IN");
```

using string constants or character pointers because they both resolve to "pointer to char."

Keep in mind that the compiler views all arrays (including string constants) as pointers.

4.12. The first thing you must ask yourself is what elements of the program have to be translated into a foreign language. The string constants must be translated. Therefore, you need a way to keep the string constants in one file and the actual working code in another file. When someone wants to translate the program, all you need to send is the file containing the string constants; the other person never has to see the source code for the program itself.

Now how do you do it? Write a simple program in the conventional manner.

```
#include <stdio.h>

main()
{
        int i;
        char buff[20];
        char *gets();

        printf("The World's Greatest Program\n");
        printf("  Copyright by Ace Grazer\n");
        printf("           1985           \n\n");

        printf("Enter a number: ");
        i = atoi(gets(buff));

        printf("\n\nThe square of %d is %d\n", i, i * i);
}
```

To remove the five string constants from the `printf()`s and place them in a separate file, you have to create a character pointer for each. Therefore, you need an "array of pointers to `chars`" (five pointers to the five different messages).

You can now write the program file (call it pf) as follows:

```
#include <stdio.h>

main()
{
        int i;
        char buff[20];
        extern char *m[];       /* Message array   */
        char *gets();

        printf(m[0]);           /* Modest title    */
        printf(m[1]);           /* Copyright notice */
        printf(m[2]);           /* Date            */

        printf(m[3]);           /* Ask for number  */
```

```
        i = atoi(gets(buff));

        printf(m[4], i, i * i);    /* Display results */
}
```

First, notice the declaration for the array of pointers, m[]. Because the messages are to be in the message file (called mf), which is separate from the pf, you must use the external storage class for the array. The declaration says that m is "an array of pointers to chars"—exactly what you need. (If you have trouble reading the declaration of m[], look at the Right-Left Rule in Chapter 6 of the *Guide*.)

Now, what does the mf look like? It appears as

```
char *m[] = {
        "The World's Greatest Program\n",
        " Copyright by Ace Grazer\n",
        "          1985          \n\n",
        "Enter a number: ",
        "\n\nThe square of %d is %d"    /* Note: no comma */
};
```

Notice that when you initialize an array, the last initializer does not have a comma after it. If you declare the array as

```
char *m[6] = {

        . . .
        /* same as before */

        . . .
};
```

there is one unused pointer. (You declared elements, but there are only five initializers.) The last pointer is not used; this unused pointer is automatically assigned a value of zero (a null pointer) and so does not point to anything useful. Read your documentation on malloc() for an example of how a null pointer can be used.

Assuming that the two files are written, you must compile the pf and mf files separately and then use the linker to merge the two. The resultant program will function the same as before.

You could have used the #include preprocessor directive to include the mf in the program. However, using the #include means that both files must be recompiled and linked whenever there is a change in either file. Recompiling both slows development. Furthermore, the mf will probably become stable sooner than will the pf, so why recompile both when only pf needs to be recompiled?

Because compile times can be quite long for large programs, the technique discussed here is valuable even if you never expect to have your program translated. Another advantage of this method is that you can "reuse" the string constants without rewriting them or increasing overhead storage (for example, use the m[3] element Enter a number: at ten different places without using additional storage for the nine repetitions).

4.13. The purpose of the question is to get you to think about program design and the use of pointers. The program is fairly simple, but do note how pointers are used.

```
#include <stdio.h>

#define CLEAR  "\014"        /* Clear screen for my terminal */
#define WRAP   16            /* Newline after this many bytes */

void memdump(), adump();

main()
{
        char buff[20], *ptr;        /* Working variables */
        int i;
        unsigned addr;
        char *gets();

        printf(CLEAR);
        printf("Enter decimal address: ");
        addr = (unsigned) atoi(gets(buff));

        printf("\nHow many memory locations: ");
        i = atoi(gets(buff));

        printf(CLEAR);
        ptr = (char *)addr;             /* Initialize pointer */
        memdump(ptr, i);                /* Display memory      */
}


/*****

        Function displays the contents of memory in
        hexadecimal, screen wraps on WRAP byte addresses

        Argument list: char *p, starting address for memory dump
                       int n, number of bytes to dump

        Return value: none
```

```
*****/

void memdump(p, n)
char *p;
int n;
{
        int i, temp, reps;
        char *atemp;                    /* Hold pointer addr */

        reps = n / WRAP;                /* Number of lines   */
        temp = n;

        do {
                for (i = 0; temp && i < WRAP; i++, temp--)
                        if (i == 0)
                                printf("%04x ", (unsigned)p + i);
                        else
                                printf("%02x ", i % 16);

                printf("\n");           /* We've printed WRAP */
                printf("   ");

                n = i;                  /* Save for ASCII     */
                atemp = p;              /* This one, too      */

                while (i--)             /* Print hex contents */
                        printf("%2x ", *p++);

                adump(n, atemp);        /* Now do in ASCII    */

                printf("\n");

        } while (reps-- > 0);           /* More left?         */
}

/*****

    Function prints what is located at ptr if it
    is a printable character; otherwise prints a ".".

    Argument list: int x        number of bytes to print
                   char *ptr    starting address

    Return value: none

*****/
```

```
void adump(x, ptr)
int x;
char *ptr;
{
        while(x--)
                if (isprint(*ptr))            /* If printable */
                        printf("%c", *ptr++);
                else {                         /* ...otherwise */
                        printf(". ");
                        ++ptr;
                }
}
```

The first part of the program defines the symbolic constants to clear the CRT screen and the number of bytes to display before starting a new line. memdump() and adump() are declared also as functions that return void.

In main(), the function asks for the starting address and assigns it to addr. The program defines addr as unsigned, because a regular int data type cannot store the higher memory addresses. The user is then asked to enter the number of bytes to be displayed (i). These two variables form the argument list for the call to memdump().

The purpose of memdump() is to display up to WRAP memory addresses on each line, followed by the hex representation of the contents at those addresses. The for loop

```
for (i = 0; temp && i < WRAP; i++, temp--)
        if (i == 0)
                printf("%04x ", (unsigned)p + i);
        else
                printf("%02x ",  i % 16);
```

causes WRAP memory addresses to be displayed, but only the first address is displayed as a 4-character address. The next 15 addresses on the line are displayed as 2-byte offsets from this base address. This was done so that there would be enough room to print the ASCII characters on the same line.

After the addresses have been printed, the function prints what is stored at those addresses. First, a newline character is printed, followed by two blank spaces to make everything line up with the respective memory addresses. Next, the function saves variable i in n (because n is no longer needed) and assigns atemp to point to the starting address to be printed. The while (i--) statement prints the hex contents for each address.

The program now calls adump() with arguments n and atemp. The purpose of adump() is to display the contents of the memory addresses in ASCII if they can be printed; otherwise, the program prints a period for the character. The adump() function calls the isprint() function, which returns logical True if the character can be printed (ASCII 32 through 126). Logical False is returned if the character at ptr cannot be printed. The while (x--) statement determines how many characters are displayed.

After the ASCII memory dump is printed by adump(), a newline is printed in memdump(). Because a do-while is used in memdump(), the function now tests reps to decide whether another pass through the do-while loop is needed. The reps variable was set by the statement

```
reps = n / WRAP;
```

and is used in the test

```
while (reps-- > 0);
```

If all repetitions have been made, the call to memdump() is complete, and the program returns to main() and terminates.

You may note three strange lines in this program

```
addr = (unsigned) atoi(gets(buff));

ptr = (char *)addr;

printf("%04x ", (unsigned)p + i);
```

The (char *) and the (unsigned) are called casts and are necessary to convert one data type to another correctly. We'll discuss casts in Chapter 6.

4.14. All you need to do is add a few lines to memdump() and add the pause() function. These changes are presented below.

```
void memdump(), adump(), pause();

void memdump(p, n)

char *p;
int n;
{
        int i, lines, temp, reps;        /* lines added here */
        char *atemp;
```

```
        reps = n / 16;
        temp = n;
        lines = 0;                    /* Set lines to zero */

        do {
                for (i = 0; temp && i < 16; i++, temp--)
                        if (i == 0)
                                printf("%04x ", p + i);
                        else
                                printf("%02x ",  i % 16);

                printf("\n");
                ++lines;            /* Increment lines here */

                printf("  ");

                n = i;
                atemp = p;

                while (i--)
                        printf("%2x ", *p++);
                adump(n, atemp);

                printf("\n");
                ++lines;                  /* Increment lines   */
                if (lines >= DEEP - 2)   /*  Need to reset it? */
                        pause(&lines);

        } while (reps-- > 0);
}
/*****
    Function pauses the screen display when the
    number of lines printed equals DEEP - 2 lines and asks
    the user to press any key to continue the display

    Argument list: int *n    pointer to number of line displayed thus far

    Return value:  none

    CAUTION:        resets line count to zero in calling function
                    and assumes CLEAR is defined

*****/

void pause(n)
int *n;
{
```

```
        printf("\nPress any key to continue: ");
        getchar();
        *n = 0;                          /* Reset line count to 0 */
        printf(CLEAR);
}
```

The only changes necessary are to declare pause() as a void
function, maintain a line counter (variable lines), increment the
counter each time a newline character (\n) is printed, and add the
pause() function. Note that when pause() is called, the program
passes the address of lines to the function to be reset. The use of
a pointer allows you to change the value of the automatic storage
class variable lines in the pause() function. The code should look
relatively simple to you by now.

4.15. The following program illustrates how a "pointer to
function" is declared.

```
#include <stdio.h>

main()
{
        char c;
        long x = 5, lfunc();
        long (*lptr)();                  /* Pointer to function */
        int i = 10, ifunc();
        int (*iptr)();                   /* Pointer to function */

        iptr = ifunc;                    /* Initialize pointers */
        lptr = lfunc;

        printf("Enter L or I: ");
        c = getchar();

        if (c == 'L' || c == 'l')
                (* lptr)(x);             /* Call the function   */
        else
                (* iptr)(i);
}


int ifunc(g)
int g;
{
        printf("\nWe called ifunc() and i = %d", g);
}
```

```
long lfunc(big)
long big;
{
        printf("\nWe called lfunc() and x = %ld", big);
}
```

The first thing to notice is how a "pointer to function" is declared. In the program line,

```
long (*lptr)();              /* Definition */
```

you defined lptr to be a "pointer to function returning long." Note that the parentheses are necessary. If you defined it as

```
long *lptr();
```

you would have a "function returning pointer to long," which is not what you want. (The Right-Left Rule discussed in Chapter 6 of the *Guide* tells how to decipher a declaration.) The parentheses enclosing the identifier (lptr) assure you that pointer is the first attribute of the declaration.

You must declare the names of any functions you want to use with pointers. If you do not, the lines

```
iptr = ifunc;                /* Initialize pointers */
lptr = lfunc;
```

will draw an error message because the compiler will consider ifunc and lfunc variable names. You have declared your functions in main(), so the compiler can initialize the pointers properly.

What is assigned into lptr when it is initialized? Just like any other variable, lfunc() is stored somewhere in memory. When lptr is initialized, the address of lfunc() is assigned to lptr. Therefore, if the *lvalue* of lfunc() is 52,000, the *rvalue* of lptr is 52,000.

Now that things are set up, you can use the "pointer to function." In the example, this was done by

```
if (c == 'L' || c == 'l')
      (* lptr)(x);           /* Call the function */
else
      (* iptr)(i);
```

If you enter the letter *l*, the function to which lptr points is called. Again, you must use the parentheses so that control is sent to the address contained in lptr. Note that the argument x is passed just as it would be in any other function call. If the function actually returned a value, you might have said

```
if (c == 'L' || c == 'l')
        x = (* lptr)(x);          /* Call the function */
else
        i = (* iptr)(i);
```

which would assign the return value from the function call to the appropriate variable (for example, x or i).

"Pointers to functions" are an advanced topic, but they can be very useful. A friend who was writing a board game had to execute a certain sequence of instructions that was determined by which square was active. He created a function and matching pointer to that function for each square on the board. Because there were 32 squares, he held all 32 pointers in an array. This was declared as

```
int (* parry[32])();
```

This line is verbalized as "an array of 32 pointers to functions returning int." All my friend had to do to execute the correct move was call the appropriate function. If a variable named move told where the player was on the board,

```
(* parry[move])();
```

would cause the appropriate function (and sequence of instructions) to execute. Once you get used to them, "pointers to functions" are easier to use than the alternative (in this case, 32 if statements).[1]

4.16. There is no difference. In both functions, s is a character array. Remember that the compiler treats all array names as pointers to the zero element (for example, s[0]).

If there is no difference, does it matter which one you use? It depends on the purpose of the function. If the function processes the array sequentially (from beginning to end or vice versa) and never has to skip around (for example, go from s[9] back to s[3] or from s[0] to s[10] and back to s[5]), it is better to declare s in the pointer form. Incrementing or decrementing pointers is usually faster than creating an index into an array. Slightly more efficient code is usually generated when pointers are used than when the declaration is in the form of an array.

---

[1] If you are interested in more information on how "pointer to function" can be used, see Chapter 2 of the *C Programmer's Library* (Purdum, Leslie, and Stegemoller, Que Corporation, 1984), which contains a detailed example and discussion of using "pointer to function" in several sorting algorithms.

Think what happens when a pointer is incremented. First, the name of the array is received in the function and becomes the *rvalue* of the variable used in the argument declaration. The function increments the *rvalue* of the pointer. After the pointer is incremented within the function, the function no longer knows where the first element of the array is. The function knows the *current rvalue* but does not know the previous *rvalue*. The function knows where the pointer now points but does not know where the pointer was (previously) pointing.

A method to return the pointer to its original value is to keep track of the number of times the pointer has been incremented, then decrement the pointer this number of times. However, the approach of using array indexes is simpler. We simply use the index to skip through the array. When we need to return to the beginning of the array, we use the index value of zero.

Therefore, you can use a pointer declaration instead of an array declaration when you process the array sequentially (either forward or backward). Use an array declaration when you expect to skip around within the array.

Most functions that receive an array as an argument can take advantage of the pointer declaration. Unless you must skip around in the array, try to use pointers in your code.

5
Input and Output

Questions about Input and Output

5.1. What are the input/output (I/O) keywords in C? *(Answer on p. 107.)*

5.2. Why doesn't C provide I/O keywords as part of the language? *(Answer on p. 107.)*

5.3. What does a #include do? How does its purpose differ from that of the linker? *(Answer on p. 107.)*

5.4. Study the following program and look for things that you might change even though the program works as is. *(Answer on p. 109.)*

```
#include <stdio.h>

main()
{
        char s[30];
        int i;

        printf("Enter your name: ");
        for (i = 0; (s[i] = getchar()) != '\n' && i < 30; ++i)
                ;

        s[i] = 0;

        printf("\nThe string is %s\n", s);

}
```

5.5. Write a function by which the user can enter from the keyboard an integer number or a string. *(Answer on p. 111.)*

5.6. Rewrite the input_() function from the previous question in order to address some of the problems with error checking which exist in that version of the function. *(Answer on p. 113.)*

5.7. The gets() function from the standard library has been used in several sample programs. Write your own gets() function. Remember that the pointer to char returned by gets() will point to the beginning of the buffer you pass to gets(), or will be a null pointer if the only character entered is EOF. Remember also that the newline is removed from the entered string. *(Answer on p. 115.)*

5.8. Depending on how you wrote the answer to 5.7, the gets() may not provide for backspacing over mistakes. Some computer operating systems automatically handle backspacing over mistakes; others do not. If your answer did not include this feature, write another version of `gets()` to handle backspacing. *(Answer on p. 117.)*

5.9. There are times when you want to require the user to enter data in a specific way. ZIP codes, state abbreviations, and dates (for example, MM/DD/YY) are common instances. In such cases, it is useful to have the prompt print a series of periods for the width of the field. Modify your `gets()` from 5.8 to print a field width as part of the prompt. *(Answer on p. 119.)*

5.10. Programs often use the ASCII bell code (a decimal 7) to call attention to an error condition in a program. What's wrong with the following program that tries to use the bell code? *(Answer on p. 122.)*

```
#include <stdio.h>

#define BELL    '\007'         /* ASCII bell code      */

main()
{
    ...                        /* Assume some code here */
    printf(BELL);

}
```

5.11. Will the following program accept a street address? (I have used the `scanf()` function.) *(Answer on p. 123.)*

```
#include <stdio.h>

main()
{
    int i;
    char s[50];
    printf("Enter street address: ");
    scanf("%d %s", &i, s);
    printf("\n\nThe number is %d and street is %s\n", i, s);
}
```

5.12. Because `scanf()` is such a versatile function, why do you need to be concerned with the other input functions (`getchar()`, `gets()`, etc.) that are usually available? *(Answer on p. 124.)*

5.13. Write a function that prints a box anywhere on the screen. You will want to take advantage of cursor addressing. (See table

5.6 in the *Guide* for the clear screen and cursor addressing codes for a number of CRTs.) *(Answer on p. 124.)*

5.14. In some situations, data must be formatted in a specific way. A common example is aligning columns of data to make the data easier to read. Often, you will want the user to select how the data is presented. Write a program that demonstrates the approach you would take in controlling data alignment. *(Answer on p. 128.)*

5.15. Some subset compilers do not support floating-point numbers (numbers with decimal fractions). Write a function that accepts a format field and an integer number and prints the integer number as a floating-point number. (If you are familiar with the PRINT USING statement in BASIC, try to make your function work in a similar fashion.) *(Answer on p. 129.)*

5.16. Write a program that uses cursor addressing to enter the date in the MMDDYY format. Use the formula for Zeller's Congruence to print the day of the week after the date is entered. The formula for Zeller's Congruence is *(Answer on p. 132.)*

$$z = (1 + d + (3 * (m + 1) / 5) + y + y / 4 - y / 100 + y / 400) \% 7$$

where

z = Zeller's index for day of the week (0 = Sunday)
d = day
m = month; if month equals 1 or 2, add 12
y = year

5.17. The solution to 5.16 is not "bulletproof." No error checking is performed on the date to see whether it is valid, and the indication that an error has occurred is not very graceful. Users prefer consistent and meaningful error indicators. This program just beeps and gives the users no clue about what they did wrong.

Write an error function to replace bell() in the program presented in 5.16. Replace the bell() function invocations with your new function to test it. *(Answer on p. 136.)*

Answers to Questions about Input and Output

5.1. There are none. All I/O in C is done through function calls.

5.2. The primary reason for not having dedicated I/O words as part of the language is the desire for flexibility. Predefined I/O keywords do not provide enough flexibility. For example, at times you may not want to display a password on the screen, or you may not want the person entering the password to be able to backspace to correct a mistake. In other situations, you do want to display (echo) the characters on the screen, as well as to have the capability of editing the input. In still other cases, you may want the input to come from a file rather than the keyboard. By using functions for I/O, programmers are free to write whatever forms they need without being limited to predefined keywords.

The standard library, of course, provides a number of functions for I/O. Earlier examples in this book used printf(), getchar(), and gets() to retrieve data and display it. Forthcoming examples will introduce other I/O functions.

A major benefit of C is that if you don't like the way a function from the standard library operates, you are free to be as creative as you wish in writing your own I/O functions.

5.3. A #include is a preprocessor directive that instructs the compiler to read a file into the source program. The general form is

```
#include "filename"
```

or

```
#include <filename>
```

When double quotation marks surround the filename, the preprocessor first searches directory of the source file. If the file is not found, the preprocessor will search whatever default directories exist. If, instead, less-than and greater-than signs (< and >) surround the filename, the preprocessor does not search the directory of the source file. Note that the order of the search may vary, depending on the compiler and the operating system. Check your documentation to learn how your compiler behaves.

For file I/O, most programs use a file named stdio.h (standard I/O header file). You have seen this file included with many programs in the previous chapters. The stdio.h file contains several variables that are essential when you are using disk data files. Instead of being written in every program that uses disk data files, these variables are placed in the standard I/O header file and #included in the program. This feature saves you typing and ensures that you won't forget some variables or misspell their names.

The following clear screen function is an example of a small header file.

```
void clrscr()              /* Clear screen function */
{
      printf("\033*");
}
```

This file is named clr.h. (Most C programmers use .h as the file name extension to indicate that the file is a header file.) Now suppose that you write the following program.

```
#include clr.h              /* Read in clrscr() */

main()
{
      clrscr();
      printf("This is a test");
}
```

The first thing that acts on a compiled program is the preprocessor. One of the primary functions of the preprocessor is to act on all the # directives in the program (for example, #define, #if, etc.).

A #include replaces itself with the contents of the file named by the #include. When the preprocessor finds the #include, it reads in the clr.h file at that point. When the preprocessor is finished, the preceding program seems to read as follows:

```
void clrscr()              /* Clear screen function */
{
      printf("\033*");
}
main()
{
      clrscr();
      printf("This is a test");
}
```

There is a difference between what is accomplished by a #include and what is done by the linker. The linker takes a function that is already compiled and merges it in the program as needed. The #include, on the other hand, takes a source code file and places that source code in the source code of the program being compiled. The linker works with code that has already been compiled, but a #include brings in source code that needs to be compiled.

The distinction is important. Each file that is #included in a program increases the time necessary to compile the program. The included file must also go through all the semantic and syntactic checks of the compiler. The linker's job is much simpler because the code has already passed through the compiler. Therefore, the linker can add a function to a program file faster than a #include can.

Which should be used? A #include is used for header files that have variables (extern storage class) and function declarations that are common to a large number of programs. However, header files normally do not contain function definitions. In fact, UNIX C programmers believe that it is "distasteful" to have any definition—variable or function—in a header file.

Instead of having #include files with function definitions, compile the functions separately, let the linker merge them into a program, and save the variables for the header files.

5.4. The same constant (30) appears several places in the program. This is a tipoff that a #define might be used.

The other thing that is misleading is the statement

```
s[i] = 0;
```

The purpose of the statement is to mark the end of the string by placing the null terminator in the s[] character array. The proper representation for a null is the character \0. Because the null equals binary zero, the program works. However, if you looked only at that line and the rest of the program were not available, it might appear that s[] was an integer array. Debugging is hard enough without being sneaky about what you are doing, so why not make the assignment more clearly reflect the intent of the statement?

A functional equivalent might be

```
#include <stdio.h>

#define MAXSTR 30              /* Max length for string     */
#define EOS    '\0'            /* Null terminator for string */

main()
{
        char s[MAXSTR];
        int i;

        printf("Enter your name: ");
        for (i = 0; (s[i] = getchar()) != '\n' && i < MAXSTR - 1; ++i)
                ;
        s[i] = EOS;

        printf("\nThe string is %s\n", s);
}
```

The program uses two #defines to define the maximum string length (MAXSTR) and the end of the string (EOS). The use of MAXSTR in the declaration of s[] and in the test in the for loop forms a visual link between the variable and the test.

Notice that the test has been modified to MAXSTR - 1. Why? The original version has an obscure bug. The declaration of s[] calls for 30 elements in the character array. Suppose that i equals 29 and that the character entered in element s[29] is not a newline (\n). Because i is less than 30 and the character was not a newline, i is incremented to 30. Now i is no longer less than 30, so the for loop ends.

The program then tries to place an EOS in s[30]. However, the character array has been declared to have 30 elements, which span s[0] through s[29], *not* s[1] through s[30]. Who knows what gets clobbered when the null character is assigned! C does not provide for boundary checks on array subscripts. Be careful about using array boundaries for logical checks. (The N-1 Rule in Chapter 4 of the *Guide* discusses array boundaries.)

Liberal use of #defines helps to make programs clearer and much easier to debug. Such #defines are often candidates for header files if the #defines are used repeatedly.

5.5. A first attempt is

```
#include <stdio.h>

#define MAXSTR 30              /* Max string length    */
#define STR       0            /* Flag for string data */
#define NUM       1            /* Flag for numeric data */
#define EOS       '\0'         /* End of string         */

main()
{
        char s[MAXSTR], c;
        int num;
        void input_();

        printf("String or number (S, N) : ");
        c = getchar();

        if (toupper(c) == 'S' )          /* String or number ? */
                input_(s, &num, STR);
        else
                input_(s, &num, NUM);

        if (toupper(c) == 'S' )
                printf("\nThe string is: %s\n", s);
        else
                printf("\nThe number is: %d\n", num);
}

/*****
        A general I/O function that can accept
        either string or numeric data

        Argument list: char buff[]        character array
                       int *ptr           pointer to integer
                       int flag           flag to indicate whether
                                          a string or number
                                              0 = string
                                              1 = number


        Return value:  none
*****/

void input_(buff, ptr, flag)
char buff[];
int *ptr, flag;
{
```

```
        int i;
        printf("\n\nEnter a ");        /* Which to get      */
        if (flag)
                printf("number: ");
        else
                printf("string: ");
                                        /* Input as a string */

        for (i = 0; (buff[i] = getchar()) != '\n'; ++i)


                ;
        buff[i] = EOS;                  /* Add null to string */

        if (flag)                       /* Numeric conversion */
                *ptr = atoi(buff);
}
```

The program begins by asking whether a string or a number is wanted. The function `toupper()` converts to an uppercase letter whatever was entered. The `if` test is needed to set the appropriate flag (STR or NUM) for the call to `input_()`.

Once inside `input_()`, the program displays a prompt for the user to enter the appropriate data type based on the value of `flag`. The `for` loop accepts the input and terminates when a newline is entered. [You could have used `gets(buff)` here, provided that you declared `gets()` to return a pointer to `char`.]

If a string is requested, the user enters the data directly in the character array passed from `main()`. (Arrays are not copied on function calls, remember?) If a number is requested, the same character array is used. If data already exists in `s[]` in `main()`, this routine will clobber the data. Assume for now that this is not a problem.

After the data is entered in the character array, the null terminator is appended to the string. If a string is requested, nothing further is done, and the program returns from the function. If a number is wanted, a call to `atoi()` (ASCII to integer) is made to convert the string to an integer data type. The program then assigns the resulting number from `atoi()` to `*ptr`. Because `*ptr` is an integer pointer that points to `num` in `main()`, indirection places the number entered in `num`. The program then displays the appropriate data that was entered on the basis of `c`'s value.

If you use this function in your library, you will probably omit the `printf()`s. Also, no error checking is performed on what is entered: the user can enter more characters than the array can hold, or the number can exceed the maximum value of an int. You must address these issues before you can consider the function "safe."

5.6. There are two things to check. First, can input_( ) exceed the length of the character array? Second, is the number entered valid data for an integer? Checks on the length of the string entered are easy. Getting valid data for an integer poses more interesting problems.

```
#include <stdio.h>

#define MAXSTR 30          /* Max string length    */
#define STR      0         /* Flag for string data */
#define NUM      1         /* Flag for numeric data */
#define EOS      '\0'      /* End of string        */

main()
{
        char s[MAXSTR], c;
        int num;
        void inputx();

        printf("String or number (S, N): ");
        c = getchar();

        printf("\n\nEnter a ");
        if (toupper(c) == 'S') {
                printf("string: ");
                inputx(s, &num, STR, MAXSTR);
        } else {
                printf("number: ");
                inputx(s, &num, NUM, MAXSTR);
        }
        if (toupper(c) == 'S')
                printf("\nThe string is: %s\n", s);
        else
                printf("\nThe number is: %d\n", num);
}

/*****
        A general I/O function that can accept
        either string or numeric data
```

```
         Argument list: char buff[]         character array
                        int *ptr            pointer to integer
                        int flag            flag to indicate whether
                                            a string or number
                                            0 = string
                                            1 = number
                        int len             maximum length of string


         Return value:  none
*****/
#define BELL                  "\007"        /* Ring bell   */


void inputx(buff, ptr, flag, len)
char buff[];
int *ptr, flag, len;
{

        int i;
                                           /* Input as a string */
                                           /* and check max len */
        for (i = 0; (buff[i] = getchar()) != '\n' &&
            i < len - 1; ++i)
                ;
        buff[i] = EOS;                     /* Add null to string */

        if (flag) {                        /* Numeric conversion */
                i = atoi(buff);

                                           /* Range check       */
                if ((i > 0 && buff[0] == '-') ||
  (i < 0 && buff[0] != '-')) {
                        printf("not valid integer data\n");
                        printf(BELL);
                        *ptr = 0;
                } else
                        *ptr = i;
        }
}
```

The program is almost identical to the program in 5.5. In the inputx() function, the for loop checks the maximum length of the string that has been passed to the function as an argument. The function stops accepting input when the maximum is reached.

Checking the integer value is more subtle. You will recall from the discussion of bit shifting that the most significant bit for a positive integer is zero and that the most significant bit for a negative integer is one. Therefore, the line

```
if ((i > 0 && buff[0] == '-') || (i < 0 && buff[0] != '-'))
```

checks to see whether the value in i is reversed from what the first character in the buffer would suggest.

If the incoming number has a value higher than the maximum integer (32,767, or 2,147,483,647 for 32-bit computers), the high bit will be on, suggesting a negative value, and i will be less than zero. However, the first character entered in buff[] will not be a minus sign, where a minus sign should occur if the number was actually negative. The opposite occurs when i is positive but the first character entered is a minus sign. If i is positive but a minus sign is the first character in buff[], the string in buff[] cannot be converted successfully to an integer.

The if test checks for either condition: i is positive, and a minus sign is the first character; or i is negative, and the first character is not a minus sign. If either condition is satisfied, the function assigns the value zero to the number.

This approach has several "holes." First, you may not enter the negative sign as the first character in the buffer. (You can enter a blank space.) Second, the manufacturer of the compiler conceivably could use some alternative way of handling integer numbers. There might be some hardware consideration that alters the way integers are stored. You would need to experiment to see whether the function works with different compilers and hardware. Finally, is assigning a value of zero to the integer a good way to indicate an error value? Your guess is as good as mine.

If it does nothing else, this approach points up some of the problems in writing generalized input routines. In most cases, extreme values for data types (numbers too big or too small or array subscripts out of bounds) tend to mess things up. Beware!

5.7.

```
#include <stdio.h>

#define MAXSTR  80        /* Max characters */
#define EOS     '\0'      /* End-of-string  */

main()
{
        char s[MAXSTR];

        char *gets();
```

```
        printf("Enter a string: ");

        gets(s);

        printf("\nThe string is %s", s);
        printf(" and this should follow on the same line\n");
}


/*****
        Function accepts a string from the terminal
        and places it in buff

        Argument list: char *buff        character array for string

        Return value:  NULL if only entered character is EOF,
                       otherwise pointer to original buff

        CAUTION:       assumes buffer large enough for string and null
*****/

char *gets(buff)
char *buff;
{

        int c;
        char *cp;

        cp = buff;

        while ((c = getchar()) != '\n' && c != EOF)
                *buff++ = c;

        *buff = EOS;

        if (cp == buff && c == EOF)    /* EOF only character entered */
                return (NULL);
        else
                return (buff);
}
```

The function is simple. cp is defined as a character pointer and is assigned the value of buff; cp and buff now point to the same address in memory.

In the while loop, the entered character is placed into c and then checked to see whether the character is a newline or EOF, the end-of-file character. If not, c is placed into the buffer pointer by buff,

buff is incremented, and the while loop continues to get more characters by calls to getchar().

When a newline or EOF is sensed, the while loop terminates without placing c into the buffer, and the function places an end-of-string in the character array. Next we have a two-part comparison. First, we compare cp with buff. cp is the copy made of the original pointer, buff. If the two pointers are equal, only a newline or EOF was entered, and c is compared against EOF. If c is equal to EOF, the only character entered was the EOF, and a null pointer is returned.

If the two pointers are equal and c is not EOF, a newline was the only entered character. If the two pointers are not equal, then other characters were entered. In either case, the function returns cp, which holds the address originally held by buff.

Notice that an asterisk has not been used in the assignment or comparison of cp and buff. When you assign the value of one pointer to another, the "contents of" operator is not used. When you copy the contents of the pointer, you copy the *rvalue* (the address the pointer holds) from one pointer to the other. When comparing pointers, you compare their *rvalues* also. When comparing pointers against each other, you test whether the two pointers hold the identical address or different addresses. In each case, you want the contents of the pointer, but not the object to which the pointer is pointing.

For example, the first part of the if test is equivalent to

```
if (cp == buff)
```

which tests whether the memory address held by cp is identical to the one held by buff. This is radically different from

```
if (*cp == *buff)
```

which tests whether the character pointed to by cp is identical to the one pointed to by buff.

5.8. The only change you need to make is to have the computer sense when a backspace or a delete character is entered. The rest of the function is the same.

```
#include <stdio.h>
#define MAXSTR    80         /* Max characters */
#define EOS       '\0'       /* End-of-string  */


main()
{
        char s[MAXSTR];
        char *gets();

        printf("Enter a string: ");
        gets(s);

        printf("\nThe string is %s", s);
        printf(" and this on same line\n");
}

/*****
        Function accepts a string from the terminal
        and places it in buff

        Argument list: char *buff       character array for string

        Return value:  NULL if only entered character is EOF,
                       otherwise pointer to original buff

        CAUTION:       assumes buffer large enough for string and null

*****/

#define DEL     '\177'       /* ASCII Delete character */
#define BACK    '\010'       /* ASCII Backspace        */

char *gets(buff)
char *buff;
{
        int c;
        char *cp;

        cp = buff;

        while ((c = getchar()) != '\n' && c != EOF)
                if (c != DEL && c != BACK)
                        *buff++ = c;
                else {
                        --buff;
                        if (c == BACK)
                                printf("%c%c", ' ', BACK);
```

```
                        else
                            printf("%c%c%c", BACK, ' ', BACK);
                    }
        *buff = EOS;                        /* Add null */

        if (cp == buff && c == EOF)
                return (NULL);
        else
                return (cp);
    }
```

As before, c is used as a temporary variable to hold the character returned from getchar(), and the while loop continues while getchar() returns a character other than a newline or EOF. Two #define constants are used in the check for a backspace (BACK) or a delete (DEL). If the entry is neither, c is assigned to the character array, and the pointer is incremented for the next character.

If the character entered is a BACK or a DEL character, the pointer is decremented so that you can "reuse" the element in the character array holding the character. The program again tests c to determine whether it is a BACK or a DEL. The printf() statements "erase" the wrong character on the screen and get ready for the corrected character.

5.9. This function is a little more difficult than it appears. (I call it getsf() for "get string with field.")

```
#include <stdio.h>

#define MAXSTR  80          /* Max characters */
#define EOS     '\0'        /* End-of-string */

main()
{
        char s[MAXSTR];
        int i;
        char *gets(), *getsf();

        printf("Width of input field ( < 20)");
        i = atoi(gets(s));

        printf("\n\nEnter a string: ");

        getsf(s, i);
        printf("\nThe string is %s\n", s);
}
```

```
/*****
          Function accepts a string from the terminal and places it
          in buff. If the function is called and width is a nonzero
          value, the function prints a series of dots on the input
          line to correspond to width of field. If wide is called
          with a value of zero, no field width is wanted.

          Argument list: char *buff      character array for string
                         int wide        width of input string

          Return value:  pointer to original buff if characters
                         entered, otherwise NULL

          CAUTION:       assumes buffer large enough for string and null
*****/

#define DEL     '\177'       /* Delete character */
#define BACK    '\010'       /* Backspace        */
#define BELL    "\007"       /* Bell code        */
#define TRUE    1            /* Logic True       */

char *getsf(buff, wide)
char buff[];
int wide;
{
        char c, space;
        int i, j;

        if (wide)                       /* Used for backspacing */
                space = '.';
        else
                space = ' ';

        while (TRUE) {
                i = wide;
                j = 0;
                if (wide) {                     /* We want a width */
                        while (i--)             /* Print dots      */
                                printf(".");

                        i = wide;
                        while (i--)             /* Go back         */
                                printf("%c", BACK);
                }
```

```
while ((c = getchar()) != '\n')
        if (c != DEL && c != BACK) {
                buff[j] = c;
                ++j;
        } else {
                --j;
                if (c == BACK)
                        printf("%c%c", space, BACK);
                else
                        printf("%c%c%c", BACK, space, BACK);
        }
        buff[j] = EOS;

        if (wide)                       /* If fixed width */
                if (strlen(buff) == wide)
                        break;
                else {
                        printf(BELL);
                        i = wide;
                        continue;
                }
        break;                  /* No width        */
}                               /* End while (TRUE) */

if(j)
        return (buff);
else
        return (NULL);
}
```

The function first sets the variable space equal to a dot or a blank space so that the appropriate character can be used when you backspace. If wide is nonzero, a field width has been given. In this case, space is set to a dot so that a dot replaces the last entered character when you backspace. A zero wide indicates that no set field width is desired, and spaces will be used when you backspace.

You then create an infinite loop with the while (TRUE) statement. The if (wide) statement causes dots to be printed after the prompt in the calling function only if a width specification is given (wide is not zero).

Another while loop calls getchar() until a newline is sensed. If a backspace or a delete is entered, the appropriate codes are printed to erase the character and backspace the cursor. Note how space is used to print dots or blank spaces. If the character is "good," it is assigned to the appropriate element in buff[]. (j does the indexing into the array.)

After a newline is entered, the null character is appended to the string. The program then checks to see whether a width specification was given. If no specification was given, the function jumps to the if(j) test. If a specification was given, a call to strlen() checks to see whether the length of the string entered equals the width specification. If the entered string is not the correct length, the program stays in the infinite while (TRUE) loop until a value equaling the right length is entered. If the string is the same length as wide, the while loop is exited.

The if(j) test checks whether one or more characters have been entered into buff. If j is nonzero, you return the address of buff. If j is zero, no character was entered, and the function returns the NULL.

Note that the use of buff differs from the way it was used in the gets() in 5.8 and allows this test. buff is declared as an array, not as a pointer. An array index (j) is used for moving through the buffer by incrementing the index. This method was chosen because the function may have to start over if the width specification doesn't match what is entered by the user. The function must "back up" to element buff[0] if an error occurs. If you do not use an array index, you first must determine where you are in the string (which is not easy) and then decrement the pointer enough times to get back to the beginning of buff[]. As mentioned in Chapter 4, pointers are great for sequential processing of arrays but not always for skipping around in arrays. Therefore, the code is simpler if buff[] is declared to be an array in this situation.

5.10. The general form for printf() is

```
printf(control string, arg1, arg2, .... argn);
```

The *control string* is usually a string constant enclosed by double quotation marks. Because the control string is a string constant, it is an array of characters, and the compiler treats it as "pointer to char."

When program control is sent to printf(), the function scans the control string, looking for the conversion character (%) in the string constant. If no conversion characters are in the control string, the program simply prints the string. This means that printf() prints out *whatever* is sent for the control string, as though it were a null-terminated array of characters.

printf() is sent an escape sequence that is a single character ('\007'). printf() expects a string and has no indication that it isn't being passed a pointer to an array of characters. printf() treats the single character as if the character were a "pointer to chars." main() is sending the character's *rvalue* ('\007'), which printf() treats as an *lvalue* (the memory address 7). The end result is that printf() prints whatever is at memory address 7, as though the data were a null-terminated array of characters. The function will march through memory, printing whatever the function finds at those addresses until it finds a binary zero.

The correction is simple: pass printf() the null-terminated string it expects. All you need do is change the #define.

```
#define BELL    "\007"    /* Now it's a string */
```

This change causes BELL to be created as a two-character array (a binary 7 followed by the null), which is exactly what printf() is expecting.

If you want to define the BELL code as a single-character constant and not an array of characters, two changes must be made. First, define the symbolic constant as a character constant:

```
#define BELL '\007'      /* Now it's a character */
```

Second, don't use printf() to print the constant; use a function designed to output a single character. Instead of printf(), use

```
putchar(BELL);
```

Keep in mind that string constants between double quotation marks resolve to "pointer to chars"; and if that's what the function is expecting, that's exactly the way the function will treat *whatever* is passed to it.

5.11. Whether the program works properly depends on the address entered. The call to scanf() asks for two arguments. The first is a street number, which is assigned to i. The second is a string for the street (s[]). If the address is

123 Daymond

variable i contains 123, and s[] contains Daymond. However, if the address is

123 East Daymond

i still contains the street number, but s[] contains only the word *East*; Daymond is lost because the function scanf() uses a blank space to terminate entry for a field. Accepting "123 East Daymond" requires changing the program definitions and scanf() to

```
char r[50];
scanf("%d %s %s", &i, s, r);
```

This code allows one street number and two strings for the full street address.

Note: Figure 5.12 in some printings of the first edition of the *Guide* is in error, and the accompanying narrative is misleading. First, in the figure, there should be no quoted string in the scanf() call. It should read

```
scanf("%s", adr);
```

Second, the text is misleading because I concentrated my comments on the length of the string and ignored the fact that my example had two blank spaces in the input string ("123 Main Street"). Obviously, the only thing contained in the string after running the program in figure 5.12 is 123 (for the reasons just discussed).

There is really nothing tricky about using scanf(). The primary rule to remember is that scanf() expects pointers for the arguments. This means that, except for arrays (which resolve to pointers anyway), variables must use the "address of" operator in the argument (for example, &i). This practice ensures that scanf() gets the *lvalue* of the variable for assignment to the input stream.

5.12. Because function scanf() can accept virtually all data types, it is an extremely complex and large function. Most versions of scanf() probably take more than 4K of code.

When you are simply asking the user to enter a string, gets() uses considerably less code. If you are working with many different data types, scanf() is more appropriate. Don't forget, however, that even if you are working with only integer data, scanf() pulls in all the floating-point (and other) support routines as well. In programs that deal with a limited variety of data types, scanf() is an "H-bomb-to-kill-an-ant" approach to the problem.

5.13. Several support functions that can be used in answering this question are also useful in their own right. Therefore, I have written the program with an eye to reusing several functions.

```
#include <stdio.h>

char *gets();              /* declare some functions */
void box(), clrscr(), cursor(), line();

main()
{
        int i, j, w, d;
        char s[10];

        clrscr();
        printf("Enter row for box: ");
        i = atoi(gets(s));

        printf("\nEnter column for box: ");
        j = atoi(gets(s));

        printf("\nEnter width (in columns): ");
        w = atoi(gets(s));

        printf("\nEnter depth (in rows): ");
        d = atoi(gets(s));

        clrscr();
        box(w, d, i, j);
}

/*****
        Function prints n repetitions of character c
        from the current cursor position. The character printed
        is contained in c.

        Argument list: int n      number of times to print character
                       char c     character to print

        Return value: none

*****/

void line(n, c)
int n;
char c;
{
        if (n < 0)             /* Just in case we goof */
                n = 0;
```

```
        while(n--)
                printf("%c", c);
}

/*****
        Function draws a box on the screen that is
        "wide" spaces wide and "deep" spaces deep. The cursor is
        set to row col, which is the upper-left corner of the box.

        Argument list:  int wide    width of box (cols)
                        int deep    depth of box (rows)
                        int row     upper-left row coordinate
                        int col     upper-left column coord

        Return value:  none

*****/

void box(wide, deep, r, c)
int wide, deep, r, c;
{

        int i, j;
        if (wide < 2)       /* Just in case we get something  */
                wide = 2;   /* strange                        */
        if (deep < 2)
                deep = 1;

        cursor(r, c);                /* Place cursor in upper-left */
        printf("+");
        line(wide - 2, '-');
        printf("+");

        for (j = 1; j < deep; ++j) {
                cursor(r + j, c);
                printf("|");
                cursor(r + j, wide + (c - 1));
                printf("|");
        }

        cursor(r + deep, c);
        printf("+");
        line(wide - 2, '-');
        printf("+");
}
```

```
/*****
        Function positions the cursor at the
        row-column coordinates given

        Argument list: int row    row coordinate
                       int col    column coordinate

        Return value:  none

        CAUTION:       values given assume ADDS Viewpoint
                       for #define
*****/

#define CURSPOS    "\033Y"       /* Leadin for ADDS */

void cursor(row, col)
int row, col;
{
        printf("%s%c%c", CURSPOS, row + 32, col + 32);
}


/*****
        Function clears the screen for the ADDS Viewpoint

        Argument list: none

        Return value:  none

        CAUTION:       values given assume ADDS Viewpoint
                       or #define
*****/

#define CLEARS      "\014"      /* Clear screen for ADDS */

void clrscr()
{
        printf(CLEARS);
}
```

The functions are fairly simple and need little explanation. The line() function can be used several ways. For example, if you use box() to draw an input window on the screen and then need to erase whatever is in the box, line() can be called with a blank space for the character to be printed. This is different from the erase-to-end-of-line feature of most CRTs because you can erase part of a line without erasing to the end of the line. This feature is useful when you want to eliminate the contents of the box but not the box itself.

The functions have been defined in such a way that they can be compiled alone and incorporated in your library. Note the use of the #defines in cursor() and clrscr(). If you change terminals, you need only to edit the #defines in both functions, recompile the functions, and then relink them into the programs. Placing the symbolic constants in the functions means that you don't need to edit the source code for the programs that use these routines.

5.14. The crux of the problem is being able to change the control string of printf() "on the fly." You need to be able to pass different control strings to printf() based on what the user selects.

Because the control string for printf() resolves to a pointer, one approach might be the following:

```
#include <stdio.h>

main()
{
        int i, number;
        char s[10]; char *gets();
        static char *field[] = {
                "%d\n",
                "%10d\n",
                "%20d\n"
        };

        number = 12345;

        printf("Do you want:");
        printf("\n1. Regular    2. Ten wide    3. Twenty wide");
        printf("\n\nEnter option: ");

        i = atoi(gets(s));

        printf(field[i - 1], number);
}
```

The key, of course, is the static character array field[]. The attribute list of field[] is "an array of pointers to chars," which is exactly what printf() needs.

If the user selects option 2 (a ten-wide field), the program uses the second element of field. Because this element is actually field[1], the final printf() uses field[i - 1] to index into the proper element of the array.

With this approach, you can pass the necessary control string to printf() without having to use a series of if statements based on string constants for several printf()s.

5.15. This function is complicated by the fact that you might need to produce numbers that are smaller than the decimal fraction. That is, if the number is 1 and you specify two decimal places, you want the function to print .01, not 1.

```
#include <stdio.h>

main()
{
        int i;
        char s[20];
        char *gets();
        void p_using();

        printf("Enter a number: ");
        i = atoi(gets(s));

        printf("\nEnter format (e.g., XXX.XX): ");
        gets(s);

        p_using(s, i);
        printf("\n\n");
        for (i = 0; i < 15; ++i) {
                p_using(s, rand());
                printf("\n");
        }

}


/*****

        Function accepts a field string telling how a
        number is to be formatted. The number is an integer but
        can be printed as a decimal fraction.

        Argument list: char *s   pointer to the format string
                       int n     the number

        Return value: none
```

```
*****/

void p_using(s, n)
char *s;
int n;
{
        int decimal, len, blanks;
        char buff[20], *ptr;
        char *itoa();

        ptr = s;                    /* Temporary pointer     */
        len = strlen(s);            /* Length of format string */
        itoa(buff, n);              /* Convert n to string   */
        decimal = strlen(buff);     /* How long is our number */
        blanks = (len - decimal) - 1; /* How many blanks?    */
        len = 0;
        while (*ptr != '.') {       /* Find the decimal point */
                ++len;              /* and save in len       */
                ++ptr;
        }

                                    /* If smaller than decimal */
                                    /* find number of blanks  */
        if ((len - blanks) <= 0) {
                len = blanks - len;
                blanks -= len;
        } else
                len = 0;
        if (blanks < 0) {           /* Number too big for field */
                printf("format error");
                exit(1);
        }
        while (blanks--) {          /* Pad with blanks as needed */
                printf("%c", ' ');
                ++s;
        }
        if (len) {                  /* If number smaller than */
            printf(".");            /* decimal field          */
                while (len--) {
                        printf("0");
                        ++s;
                }
        }
        ptr = buff;
        while (*s)                           /* Print rest of it */
                if (*s++ == '.')
                        printf("%c", '.');
```

```
                else
                    printf("%c", *ptr++);
    }
```

The function receives the format field (for example, XXXX. XX) as a "pointer to char" and the number as an int. Several working variables are then declared. Before printing the number, the program needs the number of blank spaces required; so the function determines the length of the format string (len) and the ASCII representation of the number (n) and assigns that to decimal. Then the program finds out how many blank spaces are needed and assigns that number to blanks. Because the function assumes a decimal field, blanks is adjusted for the presence of the decimal point (the - 1 in the assignment of blanks).

Because the number may occupy fewer digits than the field requests (XXXX. XX and n equal to 1), the function determines how many characters there are before the decimal point in the field. The program reuses len to hold this value. Next, len and blanks are adjusted if the number is smaller than the decimal field; otherwise, len is set to 0.

If blanks is negative, there is a format error, and the function dumps the user back to the operating system by the call to exit(). If everything is correct, the program prints the leading blanks and increments the pointer to the format string to keep everything in sync.

If the decimal field is larger than the number, len will have a nonzero value. The if (len) is executed in this case, causing a decimal point and 0 to be printed as needed. Again, s must be incremented to keep it aligned.

The while (*s) causes the rest of the number to be printed after this process is accomplished. In the sample program, the user enters the number and the format field. After that number is printed, the program calls an integer random-number generator to print a few more numbers using the function.

Such a function can be useful for subset compilers that support the long data type but not floating-point numbers. For example, if you think of everything in pennies instead of dollars, the function can be used in small accounting applications. In situations where decimal fractions are multiplied, care must be taken to ensure that the position of the decimal point is properly reflected in the format field.

A couple of functions may be new to you in this program. itoa() is a function that converts an integer to an ASCII string, the opposite of atoi(). rand() is a function that returns a random integer number. Most compilers provide a rand() function, although its name may be different. Some compilers provide an itoa() or compariable function with a different name. You will need to check your compiler's documentation for the function that converts an integer number to an ASCII string.

If you do not have an integer-to-ASCII function, you can use a form of printf() called sprintf(). Use

```
sprintf(buff, "%d", n);
```

in place of

```
itoa(buff, n)
```

5.16. This task is best broken down into several smaller functions. I have assumed that you have cursor addressing, clear screen, and bell functions available from earlier programs.

```
#include <stdio.h>

void clrscr(), cursor(), bell();
void getdate();
main()
{
        char c;
        int i;

        clrscr();                    /* Clear screen */
        getdate(10, 20);
}


/*****

        Function gets the month, day, and year. We assume the
        maximum valid year is 1999, which also means that we
        limit valid years to the 20th century.

        Argument list: int row   row position
                       int col   column position

        Return value:  none

        CAUTION:       valid only 1900-1999
```

```
*****/

#define MAXYEAR        99

void getdate(row, col)
int row, col;
{
        int i, month, day, year;
        char c, s[10];
        static char *d[] = {"Sunday", "Monday", "Tuesday",
                "Wednesday", "Thursday", "Friday", "Saturday" };
        cursor(row, col);

        printf("__:__:__");                     /* Field template */

        month = get_two(0, 12, row, col);       /* Get month */
        day = get_two(0, 31, row, col + 3);     /* Get day   */
                                                /* Get year  */
        year = get_two(0, MAXYEAR, row, col + 6);

        i = zeller(month, day, year);   /* Zeller's Congruence */

        cursor(row, col + 10);
        printf("(%s)", d[i]);                   /* Print is */
}
/*****

    Function accepts two digits from the keyboard. It
    will accept no more and no less than two digits.

    Argument list: int low       lower bound for number
                   int high      upper bound for number
                   int row       row position for input
                   int col       column position

    Return value: int value      the number entered

*****/

#define TRUE        1

int get_two(low, high, row, col)
int low, high, row, col;
{
        int i, value;
        char c, s[5];
```

```
        cursor(row, col);
        i = 0;
        while (TRUE) {                  /* Keep at it until   */
                                        /* they do it right   */
                c = getchar();
                if (isdigit(c)) {       /* Was it a digit?    */
                        s[i] = c;
                        ++i;
                } else {                /* If not, complain   */
                        i = 0;
                        bell();
                        cursor(row, col); /* ...and do it over */
                }

                if (i == 2) {           /* Got two digits?    */
                        value = atoi(s);
                                        /* Are they in range? */
                        if (value > low && value <= high)
                                break;
                        else {          /* If not, complain   */
                                i = 0;
                                bell();
                                cursor(row, col);
                        }
                }
        }                               /* End while(TRUE)    */

        return (value);                 /* Send it back       */
}


/*****

    Function determines the day of the week using
    Zeller's Congruence. It calculates an index for the day
    of the week where 0 is Sunday.

    Argument list:  int month       input month
                    int day         input day
                    int year        input year as two-digit number

    Return value:   int sum         index for day of week

    CAUTION:        valid only for CENTURY
```

```
*****/

#define CENTURY    1900           /* Assume 20th century   */

int zeller(month, day, year)
int month, day, year;                **
{
        unsigned sum;

        if (month < 3)               /* Offset for Jan and Feb */
                month += 12;

        year += CENTURY;             /* Add century to year    */
        sum = 1 + day + (month * 2) + ((3 * (month + 1)) /5)
          + year + (year / 4) - (year / 100) + (year / 400);
        sum %= 7;                    /* Mod it for index       */
        return (sum);
}
```

The program contains no real surprises. There are several places, however, where it uses operators that have not yet been discussed in the *Guide*. An example is in zeller(). The operator

```
month += 12;
```

is equivalent to

```
month = month + 12;
```

The general form for such operators is

variable (operator)= expression;

These operators can also be thought of as

variable = variable (operator) expression;

A complete list of the operators that can be expressed in this shorthand form is presented in table 7.1 in the *Guide*. Note that each involves an assignment to a variable after a binary operator has been used.

The isdigit() function in get_two() is typically a standard library function that returns a nonzero value if the character is an ASCII digit, or zero if the character is not an ASCII digit. The test

```
if (isdigit(c))
```

works as if isdigit() returned a logical True (1) value. The if statement tests the expression inside the parentheses for a nonzero value. If c is a digit, isdigit() returns a nonzero value, and the statement block for the if is executed. If c is not a digit, isdigit() returns a value of zero, and the statement block associated with the else statement is executed.

The comments with the code should explain what is going on within each function for the rest of the program.

5.17. Several design considerations must be made. First, how can you provide consistent error messages? A step in the right direction is to use one area of the screen for all error messages. Some CRTs and video screens have a 25th row (the status line) that can be used for error messages. If your CRT or video screen does not have a status line, pick some other section of the display where messages will not interfere with the normal I/O of the program. In most applications, columns 50 through 80 of row 1 are a good choice. Whatever section of the display you select, write the rest of the program so that it does not interfere with the "error window."

Second, how do you provide meaningful error messages? In my opinion, a meaningful error message is one that conveys the nature of the problem and can be read at a glance. If additional details are needed, the documentation for the program should explain those details. Meaningful error messages are *not* error numbers. Users get unpleasant when they have to look up numbers.

The following function is a first step toward meeting these objectives.

```
/*****

     Function prints an error message in the error window.
     The message printed is determined by the argument
     passed to the function.

     Argument list: int num          error to be printed

     Return value:  none

     CAUTION:       Several #defines establish the environment
                    in which the errors are printed. Some
                    are hardware dependent.
```

```
*****/

#define ECOL    50              /* Column for error messages */
#define EROW    1               /* Row for error messages    */
#define WIDE    79              /* CRT width minus one        */
#define DELAY   65000           /* Delay value for loop       */
#define BELL    "\007"          /* ASCII bell code            */


void perror(num)
int num;
{
        unsigned time;

        printf(BELL);                   /* Sound bell          */
        cursor(EROW, ECOL);             /* Go to error window */

        time = DELAY;                   /* For delay loop      */

        switch(num) {
                case 1:
                        printf("Not valid digit");
                        break;
                case 2:
                        printf("Value too high");
                        break;
                case 3:
                        printf("Value too low");
                        break;
                default:
                        break;
        }
        while (time--)                  /* Time to read it */
                ;                       /* Null statement */
        time = WIDE - ECOL;             /* How many blanks */

        cursor(EROW, ECOL);             /* In error window */

        while (time--)
                printf("%c", ' ');
}
```

The function is quite simple. The #defines establish the row (EROW) and column (ECOL) for the error window. WIDE defines the display's width, which is one less than the actual 80 columns available. The reason for this is that some CRTs automatically send a CR-LF combination when something is printed in the last (80th) column position. Therefore, 29 characters are available for error messages.

The DELAY symbolic constant is used to delay the program so that the error message can be read before it is erased. The actual value used depends primarily on the clock speed of the CPU. This approach is not portable, but it is easy to implement. An alternative is to set an error flag when an error occurs and to test the flag after each input is made. If the error flag is set, you need to erase the error window and reset the error flag. This also means, however, that the error message stays on the screen until the next input is reached.

Once inside the function, the program positions the cursor at the start of the error window and sounds the bell. The error message selected is determined by the num argument passed to the function as part of a switch statement. It is always a good practice to use the default case even though it is not necessary. This practice provides a known exit point if there is no case match. The break statement sends control out of the switch.

The while loop is then executed; it simply provides a few seconds for the error message to be read. The cursor is then repositioned, and the error message is erased.

Two features make the approach presented less than optimal. First, the use of string constants in the function limits it. Using pointers to the messages and storing the messages in another file would make the function more flexible.

Second, using a timing loop is never a good idea, especially when you want your code to be portable to other hardware environments. C compilers on computers that have a real-time clock (an internal clock that provides the actual date and time) usually provide a function called time(). It returns the number of seconds since an established date. The return value is usually a long int, but the return data type may vary among computers. Not all computers, however, have a real-time clock. Therefore, compilers on these computers will not have a time() function.

The program's saving grace is that this approach is simple and easy to change. If you are writing programs for just yourself, this approach should serve your purpose.

You should experiment with the perror() function and try your hand at some of the suggested improvements. A more generalized function would be a worthwhile addition to your library.

6
Other Data Types

Questions about Other Data Types

6.1. What new data types are presented in Chapter 6 of the *Guide*? Give a brief description of the distinguishing features of each. *(Answer on p. 143.)*

6.2. Write a program that shows how much storage is allocated to each data type discussed so far. An added touch would be to use an array of each data type and to show the memory locations. *(Answer on p. 143.)*

6.3. In the discussion of binary operators and mixed data types in Chapter 6 of the *Guide*, Rule 4 states that `float` variables are promoted to `doubles` before an arithmetic operation is performed. The reason is that C performs arithmetic only on resolved data types—that is, a data type that needs no conversion. (See Chapter 1 of the *C Programmer's Library*.) Because of this fact, what are the advantages and disadvantages of the `float` data type? *(Answer on p. 145.)*

6.4. Write a program that compares the times needed to multiply, on the one hand, two `float` variables and, on the other, two `double` variables. Use a loop to repeat the multiplications, and have enough loops to time the process. What are your conclusions? *(Answer on p. 145.)*

6.5. Write a program that has the user input the number of `doubles` to be used and then fills those `doubles` with a `for` loop and prints them. (Hint: This program must request storage at run time because the amount is unknown at compile time. Check the `calloc()` function in your library.) *(Answer on p. 147.)*

6.6. Euclid developed a number of algorithms still used today; one of these finds the greatest common divisor (gcd). The gcd algorithm finds the largest factor common to two numbers. For example, the gcd for 225 and 15 is 15; 15 is the largest factor by which both numbers are evenly divisible. The algorithm states: For two numbers x and y, divide x by y and assign the remainder to r. If r equals 0, y is the gcd. If r is not equal to 0, assign y into x and r into y and repeat until r equals 0.

Write a program that inputs two `long` numbers and finds the gcd of those numbers. *(Answer on p. 150.)*

6.7. Describe the general form of the ternary operator. What makes it different from the other operators? *(Answer on p. 154.)*

6.8. Most programmers are familiar with the truth tables associated with logical AND and logical OR. Write a program that first asks users which truth table they want to see and then displays the correct table. Although this can be done by simply printing the tables, design the program to use the ternary operator to set the logical result produced in each table. *(Answer on p. 155.)*

6.9. Write a function that converts a floating-point number to a dollar value with commas in the correct places in the number—for example, 1234 as $1,234.00. If you wish, make the dollar sign optional as part of the function call's argument list. *(Answer on p. 157.)*

6.10. Most full C compilers supply a number of transcendental and other floating-point library functions. Look through those functions to see whether any may be useful in calculating a monthly loan repayment. The equation is

$$\text{monthly payment} = \frac{a * i}{1 - 1 / (1 + i)^m}$$

where

  a = amount of loan
  i = monthly interest rate
  m = number of months for loan

(Answer on p. 161.)

6.11. "If a series of integer numbers begins with 1 and ends with x, the sum of the series squared equals the sum of the cubes of the same series." Write a program that inputs the ending value of the series (x) and verifies the preceding statement. *(Answer on p. 163.)*

6.12. What is a typedef in C? Give an example of how it can be used. *(Answer on p. 165.)*

6.13. A student once said that he saw little difference between a #define and a typedef and offered the following example:

```
typedef int FLAG;
FLAG flag;
```

which can be replaced with

```
#define FLAG int;
FLAG flag;
```

Is the student correct? How would you answer him? *(Answer on p. 166.)*

6.14. Give examples of initialization of a character array, an integer array, a character pointer to a message, and a two-dimensional array. What impact does storage class have on the way arrays are initialized? *(Answer on p. 166.)*

Answers to Questions about Other Data Types

6.1. A short int is a signed integer number, the range of which is determined by the compiler and the computer environment. On most micro- and minicomputers, a short is the same as an int. Some implementations make a short int the same size as a char (8 bits). On some mainframe machines, however, an int is a 32-bit number, and a short is a 16-bit number (the same range as an int on smaller systems).

A long int is a signed integer number (usually 32 bits), the range of which is from -2,147,483,648 through 2,147,483,647. On most 32-bit systems, a long int is the same size as an int.

An unsigned int is an integer number that can assume only positive values. It is the same size as an int. For 16-bit integers, an unsigned int ranges from 0 through 65,535. On 32-bit systems, the range of an unsigned int is from 0 to 4,294,967,295.

An unsigned char is a character that can have only positive values. The typical char is based on 8 bits. The range of an 8-bit char is from -128 through 127. An 8-bit unsigned char has a range from 0 through 255.

An unsigned short int and an unsigned long int are also integer numbers that can have only positive values. An 8-bit unsigned short has a range from 0 through 255, the same as an 8-bit unsigned char. A 16-bit unsigned short has a range from 0 through 65,535, the same as a 16-bit unsigned int. An unsigned long based on a 32-bit long has a range from 0 to 4,294,967,295.

A float is a 32-bit floating-point number. A float normally has 6 digits of precision.

A double is a 64-bit floating-point number. A double normally has 14 digits of precision, although some compilers have greater precision.

6.2. The following program could be written without the sizeof operator. However, the sizeof operator returns an integer that is equal to the number of bytes required to store the item specified. (The sizeof operator is discussed in Chapter 7 of the *Guide*.)

```
include <stdio.h>
main()
{
    char c[4];
    int i[4];
    unsigned u[4], j;
    long l[4];
    float f[4];
    double d[4], *ptr[4];

    printf("              A0      A1      A2      A3    Length\n");
    printf("    char      ");      /* char */
        for(j = 0; j < 4; ++j)
            printf("%u      ", &c[j]);      /* memory locations */
        printf("%d\n", sizeof(char));

    printf("    int    ");         /* int */
    for(j = 0; j < 4; ++j)
        printf("%u    ", &i[j]);          /* memory locations */
    printf("%d\n", sizeof(int));

    printf("    unsigned    ");      /* unsigned */
    for(j = 0; j < 4; ++j)
        printf("%u    ", &u[j]);      /* memory locations */
    printf("%d\n", sizeof(unsigned));

    printf("      long    ");       /* long */
    for(j = 0; j < 4; ++j)
        printf("%u    ", &l[j]);      /* memory locations */
    printf("%d\n", sizeof(long));

    printf("      float    ");       /* float */
    for (j = 0; j < 4; ++j)
        printf("%u    ", &f[j]);      /* memory locations */
    printf("%d\n", sizeof(float));

    printf("    double    ");       /* double */
    for (j = 0; j < 4; ++j)
        printf("%u    ", &d[j]);      /* memory locations */
    printf("%d\n", sizeof(double));

    printf("    pointer    ");       /* pointer */
    for (j = 0; j < 4; ++j)
        printf("%u    ", &ptr[j]);      /* memory locations */
    printf("%d\n", sizeof(ptr[1]));
}
```

This program displays a table heading followed by the data type being used. In each case, a for loop prints the memory locations of four elements of the array. Next, the program uses the sizeof operator to display the number of bytes used to store one element of the array (that is, the size of the basic data type).

It would be fairly simple to calculate the sizes of the elements by subtracting the memory addresses for two elements of the array.

The layout of the program is designed for a C compiler that uses 16-bit addresses. This layout works well for either 8-bit or 16-bit computers because the array addresses printed will be 4 or 5 digit numbers. Users of 32-bit systems may need to change the spacing in the program so that the headings (A0, A1, . . .) line up over the numbers. The array addresses on a 32-bit system may be up to 10 digits long because these systems can address gigabytes (billions of bytes) of memory space.

6.3. The float data type has two disadvantages. First, float has restricted precision. Floating-point numbers are common in a wide variety of applications, ranging from accounting to statistics; and in many cases, six digits of precision are simply not enough. Second, because arithmetic operations on floats are done in double precision, each float variable must be converted to a double before it can be used in an arithmetic expression. The conversion takes both code space and execution time.

Given these limitations, why use a float? In situations where the limited precision is sufficient and relatively few arithmetic operations are performed on the data, a float may be appropriate. One advantage is that a float requires only half the storage of a double. This can be important if you need a large array of floating-point numbers. Also, because a float is smaller than a double, the CPU has to move only half as many bytes if the data is being just "shuffled around" (for example, entered by a user and then written to disk).

Evaluate the trade-offs before you select the data type that is best for your specific situation.

6.4. The results of this experiment will vary widely according to the hardware and software. Hardware variations are due to different processors, clock speeds, and the like. Software variations exist because of differences in the use of floating points and optimizers, and (in many cases) because of restrictions the hardware places on the software.

With my hardware and software, the following program ran in approximately 3.8 seconds, using the double data type, and in 4.1 seconds, using the float data type. (The float conversions took some time, but not much.) The same program under a different compiler took just over 12 seconds for both tests, with a fraction of a second in favor of the double. Because compilers (and the hardware that they run on) vary considerably, you may have to change the value of LOOP to get meaningful measurements.

```c
#include <stdio.h>

#define DOUBLE  1               /* Do double or float    */
                                /* 0 = float, 1 = double */
#define LOOP    1000            /* Number of iterations  */
#define BELL    "\007"          /* Bell code             */

#if DOUBLE
        double x, y, sum;       /* DOUBLE = 1            */
#else
        float x, y, sum;        /* DOUBLE = 0            */
#endif

main()
{
        unsigned i;

        i = LOOP;
        sum 2 0.0;              /* Make sure floating point */
        x = y = .5;

        printf(BELL);           /* Start timing          */
        while (i--)
                sum = sum + x + y;

        printf(BELL);           /* End timing            */
        printf("%f", sum);
        printf("\nThe size of sum = %d", sizeof(sum));
}
```

Not all compilers allow the #if preprocessor directive. The #if construct

```c
#if DOUBLE
        double x, y, sum;       /* DOUBLE = 1            */
#else
        float x, y, sum;        /* DOUBLE = 0            */
#endif
```

translates: If DOUBLE is logical True (its value is not 0), compile the statements that are between the #if and the #else. Because the sample program defines DOUBLE to be 1 in this case, the double definitions are compiled into the program. If the #define DOUBLE were 0, the double definitions would be skipped and the float definitions compiled. In either case, the #endif marks the end of the #if-#else directive.

If your compiler does not support the #if-#else preprocessor directive, simply compile separate versions for the double and float data types.

Keep in mind that conversions are necessary for certain data types (for example, char, short, float, function, and array), and these conversions do take time and code space. If your program performs many floating-point calculations, you may want to make the variables the double data type.

6.5. The major tasks of the program are to find out how much storage is needed for the doubles designated by the user, to get the necessary storage from the operating system, stuff the doubles into the storage, then print the doubles to see whether the program worked. Only the second task may seem a bit strange; you have already performed tasks similar to the first, third, and fourth.

```c
#include <stdio.h>

#define BELL    "\007"      /* ASCII Bell code */

main()
{
        char buff[20];
        int i, j;
        double *ptr, *base;          /* Pointers to doubles */
        char *gets(), *calloc();

        printf("Enter number of doubles needed: ");
        i = atoi(gets(buff));

        base = ptr = (double *) calloc(i, sizeof(double));

        if (!base) {
                printf("\n\nOut of memory %s", BELL);
                exit();
        }
```

```
        for (j = 0; j < i; ++j)
            *ptr++ = (double)j;

        for (j = 0; j < i; ++j, ++base)
            printf("%6.2f ", *base);
    }
```

The program first prompts the user to enter the number of `doubles` desired. This number is converted to an integer and assigned to `i`. The next statement, which does most of the work in the program, will be discussed as three distinct parts.

```
base = ptr = (double *) calloc(i, sizeof(double));
                 (3)        (1)
                                  (2)
```

Expression 1 is the function call to `calloc()`, which is a function that dynamically allocates memory storage. The function definition of `calloc()` is

```
char *calloc(nelem, nsize)
```

where `nelem` is the number of items to be stored, and `nsize` is the size of each item in bytes.

Expression 2, the `sizeof` operator, has been used for `nsize`. On some computers a `double` is 8 bytes large, and it can use the literal 8 instead of `sizeof(double)`. However, other computers may have a `double` of a different size. The `sizeof` operator guarantees that the right number of bytes for a `double` will return when expression 1 is resolved, regardless of the computer system. Using the `sizeof` operator this way helps to make the program portable.

The value returned from the call to `calloc()` is either a pointer to the amount of storage requested or zero. Because a pointer with a value of zero is not a valid pointer, `calloc()` will return a zero if the request for storage is not satisfied.

Notice that `calloc()` returns a "pointer to `char`." We must declare that the `calloc()` returns a `char *`. Otherwise, the return value from the call to `calloc()` will be treated as if it were an `int`, which is the default data type returned from a function call. In keeping with the Right-Left Rule, the declaration near `main()` tells the program that `calloc` is a *"function returning pointer to `char`."*

If the request for storage *is* satisfied, `calloc()` returns a "pointer to `char`." But that's not what you want. You want to store `doubles`. Therefore, you have to "reshape" the `char` pointer returned from calloc() into a "pointer to doubles." This is the purpose of a *cast* operator. Note the use of the cast in expression 3 of the statement

```
base = ptr = (double *)calloc(i, sizeof(double));
            (3)       (1)            (2)
```

If you collapse expression 1 and ignore the assignment operators, you can view the statement above as though it were

```
double *calloc();
```

The Right-Left rule tells us that the cast changes calloc() to a "function returning pointer to double." Because the cast operator changes the context in which the return value is used in the program, you can safely assign the pointer returned from calloc() into ptr and base, both of which are pointers to doubles. Without the cast, the increment operators used later in the program will be scaled to the size of a char, not a double. All kinds of weird things may happen. Using the cast ensures that base and ptr are assigned a "pointer to doubles."

Next the program executes

```
if (!base) {
        printf("\n\nOut of memory %s", BELL);
        exit();
}
```

to see whether calloc() satisfied the request for storage. If base does not have a valid pointer address (that is, base equals zero), the program should inform the user and abort the program. Therefore, !base provides the correct logic to execute the error message and abort the program. The exit() function returns the user to the operating system. (Enter some very large values for i to verify that this routine works as it should.)

The program now uses a for loop to fill with doubles the storage returned from calloc(). Again, note the use of the cast. Because j is an int and you want doubles, the program casts the value of j into a double before assigning the value to the storage allocated for the doubles. The postincrement on ptr moves to the following double for the next iteration of the for loop.

```
for (j = 0; j < i; ++j)
        *ptr++ = (double) j;

for (j = 0; j < i; ++j, ++base)
        printf("%6.2f ", *base);
```

Finally, a second `for` loop prints the `doubles` to show that everything worked properly. The `base` is used instead of `ptr` because `ptr` has been incremented beyond the starting point of the `doubles`, but `base` has remained at the initial value returned from `calloc()`. (An alternative is another `for` loop to decrement simultaneously `j` and `ptr` until `j` is zero. I believe that the approach just shown is clearer.)

The storage allocator functions—`calloc()` and `malloc()`—are quite useful and give you a way to allocate variables dynamically at run time. (These functions can be used to simulate a DIM A[X] statement in BASIC.) Keep in mind that the storage allocators return "pointer to `char`," so you must use a cast if the storage is to be used with some other data type.

For those using certain computer systems (typically 32-bit computers), `calloc()` automatically performs an additional function that you might not have considered. Some machines require that certain data types be located only in particular memory locations. For example, on VAX computers, the first byte of a `float` or `double` must be on an even memory address. This positioning is called *alignment;* the `float` or `double` must be on a properly aligned memory boundary. The fact to remember is that `calloc()` takes care of any necessary alignment. You do not need to worry about what `calloc()` will store. It will always return a pointer that, when properly cast, can store any data type.

For more information on `calloc()` or `malloc()`, consult your compiler's library documentation.

6.6. The question gives you a chance to implement a verbal statement of an algorithm and also gives you experience working with the `long` data type.

Using a "sideways" refinement of program design, our first steps might be

1. Initialization

    Declare working variables

2. Input

    Get the two `long` numbers (new function)

3. Processing

    Find the gcd as a `long` (new function)

4. Output

   Display gcd

5. Termination

   Nothing special

The task is fairly simple. You need two new functions, both of which use the long data type. Both functions must be declared as working variables in step 1. Both return a long (but int is the default data type returned from a function call), so both functions must be declared in main().

Furthermore, because the user enters the numbers, you need a function that converts an ASCII representation of the number into a long. Most standard libraries have an atol() that does this; but if you don't have an atol(), you can use atoi() and cast the result to a long. Obviously, though, the values of these entered int numbers will be more limited than if they were longs.

After the numbers have been entered, they must be passed to the gcd() function, which implements the gcd algorithm. This step (3) is a little more involved. Consider the statement of the algorithm:

For two numbers x and y, divide x by y and assign the remainder to r. If r equals 0, y is the gcd. If r is not equal to 0, assign y into x and r into y and repeat until r equals 0.

A first attempt to solve the problem might be as follows:

divide x by y, assign remainder to r	`start:    r = x % y;`
if r equals 0, y is gcd	`if (r == 0)` `    y = gcd;`

if r not 0, assign y into x assign r into y	`else {`
	`    x = y;`
	`    y = r;`
	`}`

repeat until r is zero	`goto start;`

The left side of the preceding figure gives the the algorithm; the right side translates the algorithm into C. Rarely does the first representation of the algorithm end up being the final form of the function, and this first version is no exception.

Because there is a loop (the start-goto), you should be able to rewrite the function without the goto. First, you need to know what ends the loop. Inspection shows that the gcd is known when the value of the remainder (r) is zero. The value of r is determined only by a modulo divide of x by y. Therefore, you need a loop controlled by r, in which r is set by the modulo divide of x by y. Because no value needs to be initialized, a while loop seems logical. You can now refine your first attempt as follows:

```
start:    r = x % y;               while (r = x % y) {

          if (r == 0)
              y = gcd;
          else {
              x = y;                   x = y;
              y = r;                   y = r;
          }                        }
          goto start;
```

The statements on the right side of this second figure show a "sideways" refinement of the statements on the left side of the figure. The refinement is much simpler than the first attempt. For instance, the statement

```
while (r = x % y)
```

replaces

```
r = x % y;
if (r == 0)
      y = gcd;
else
```

The while also gets rid of the goto and its label.

Checking the logic of the refined algorithm statement in C against the verbal statement of the algorithm seems to indicate that the refinement will work. Only after the preceding steps have been performed are you ready to write the actual code. One solution to the gcd problem follows.

```
/* Find Greatest Common Divisor for two numbers */

#include <stdio.h>

main()
{
        char buff[20];
        long num1, num2;
        long getnum(), gcd();    /* Let main() know they   */
                                 /* return long data types */
```

```
        num1 = getnum(1);        /* function to get longs */
        num2 = getnum(2);

        printf("\nGreatest Common divisor is
            %ld\n", gcd(num1, num2));
}


/*****

    Function prints a prompt in preparation to
    getting a long number

    Argument list: int val          which number; used as
                                     part of prompt

    Return value:  long             returned by atol()
                                     on number entered
                                     by user

*****/

long getnum(val)
int val;
{
        char buff[20];
        long atol();                 /* Must tell it about */
        char *gets();                /* atol() and long    */

        printf("Enter number %d ", val);

        return (atol(gets(buff)));
}

/*****

    Function used to find the greatest common divisor
    of two numbers

    Argument list: long x            first input number
                   long y            second input number

    Return value:  long y            the gcd

*****/

long gcd(x, y)
long x, y;
{
```

```
long rem1;

while (rem1 = x % y) {
        x = y;
        y = rem1;
}

return(y);
}
```

The program contains no surprises. The main error to guard against is forgetting to let the calling function know that return values from the functions getnum(), atol(), and gcd() are the long data type. As usual, gets() has also been declared.

6.7. The general form of the ternary operator is

expression 1 ? expression 2 : expression 3

If *expression 1* is logical True, *expression 2* is evaluated. If *expression 1* is logical False, *expression 3* is evaluated. Note that a single ternary evaluates either *expression 2* or *expression 3*, but never both. It can be seen, therefore, that the ternary operator is a shorthand form of the if-else construct.

```
if (expression 1)
      expression 2;
else
      expression 3;
```

The ternary operator is somewhat unusual because it uses three operands.

A common use of the ternary is to set a flag variable based on the value of some other variable, for example,

```
flag = (x > 5) ? 1 : 0;
         (1)    (2)  (3)
```

(The numbers in parentheses represent the expression numbers of the ternary.) If x is greater than 5, expression 1 evaluates to logical True and assigns a value of 1 into flag. If x is 5 or less, the expression is logical False, and flag is assigned the value of 0.

If the same example is used with if-else form, the equivalent of the ternary is

```
if (x > 5)
    flag = 1;
else
    flag = 0;
```

The ternary operator may seem strange at first, but as you become familiar with it, you will find its conciseness useful.

6.8. The following program is artificially complex, and the task could be accomplished more directly. The program does, however, use the ternary operator to set the logical result in the table.

```
/* Program to display logical AND and OR truth tables */

#include <stdio.h>

#define TRUE 1

main()
{
        int i;
        char c;
        void bell(), table();
                                        /* Which one */
        while (TRUE) {
                printf("Select a logical operator");
                printf("\n1. &&    2. ||\n");
                i = getchar() - '0';
                if (i > 0 && i < 3)
                        break;
                bell();
        }

        table(i);                       /* Print it */

}

/*****

        Function prints a logical AND or
        logical OR truth table. The table selected is determined
        by num.

        Argument list: int num        the truth table wanted
                                       1 = AND, 2 = OR
        Return value: none

*****/
```

```
void table(num)
int num;
{
        int i;

        printf("\n\nLogical ");
        (num == 1) ? printf("AND") : printf("OR");

        printf("\n\nF F | F\n");              /* Row 1 for both */

        for (i = 2; i < 4; ++i) {
            switch(i) {
                case 2:
                        printf("F T | ");
                        (num == 1) ? printf("F") : printf("T");
                        break;
                case 3:
                        printf("T F | ");
                        (num == 1) ? printf("F") : printf("T");
                        break;
            }
            printf("\n");
        }
        printf("T T | T\n");                  /* Row 4 for both */
}
```

The program begins by asking the user which table to display. The `while` loop forces the user to enter either *1* or *2* in response to the input prompt. Because there are only two choices, the function simply subtracts the *character* '0' from the character digit entered instead of calling `atoi()` to convert the character to an integer. [The `bell()` function has been used in previous examples.]

The `table()` function is based on the fact that the first and last entries in the logical AND and OR tables are the same: rows 1 and 4 in both tables are identical. Only rows 2 and 3 vary.

Logical AND	Logical OR	Row
F F ∣ F	F F ∣ F	1
F T ∣ F	F T ∣ T	2
T F ∣ F	T F ∣ T	3
T T ∣ T	T T ∣ T	4

The first use of the ternary selects the heading for the table to be printed.

```
(num == 1) ? printf("AND") : printf("OR");
```

If the user enters 1, the AND heading is printed because the first expression (num == 1) is logical True; otherwise, OR is printed. The function then prints row 1 of the table, which is the same for either table.

A for loop is used to print the next two rows (note the initial value of i). Once inside the for loop, a switch is used to select the row to be printed. On the first pass through the for loop, case 2 is selected, and the first part of the row is printed. Because the *results* of the logic test are different, however, a ternary is used to evaluate num to decide which result to print for the logic table selected.

After each case of the switch is processed, a newline is printed so that the next row starts on a new line. Similar logic (within the for and the switch) is used to decide what to print for row 3 of either table. After row 3 is processed, the for loop ends. Because row 4 is invariant, it is simply printed and the program ends.

6.9. Some detractors of C say that the language is weak because it lacks string-handling facilities. This is somewhat like saying, "I haven't shot myself in the left foot lately, so I must not be using my gun often enough." One of the strengths of C is the absence of predefined (that is, rigid) language constructs. C programmers are free to use whatever suits them, not what suits the language.

The answer to this question shows one way the problem can be addressed, but you have the freedom to design whatever best suits your needs.

```
/* Format floating-point dollar number with commas and    */
/* optional dollar sign                                    */

#include <stdio.h>

#define EOS '\0'

main()
{
        char buff[30], c;
        int dollar;
        double num, atof();
        char *gets();

        printf("Enter a number: ");         /* Get number */
        num = atof(gets(buff));
```

```
        printf("\nShould it be in dollars (Y, N):");
        c = getchar();
        dollar = (c == 'Y' || c == 'y') ? 1 : 0;

        comma(num, buff, dollar);

        printf("\n\nThe number is %s\n", buff);
}

/*****

    Function takes a floating-point dollar amount
    and places commas in the appropriate places. A leading
    dollar sign can precede the number as an option.

    Argument list: char buff[]       place to put result
                   int bucks         1 = $, 0 = no $
                   double num        dollar f.p. number

    Return value: none

*****/

void comma(num, buff, bucks)
char buff[];
int bucks;
double num;
{
        char new[50];
        int i, j, dec, len;

        j = dec = 0;
        ftoa(buff, num, 2, 'f');

        while (buff[j])              /* Find the decimal      */
                if (buff[j] == '.')
                        dec = j++;
                else
                        j++;

        ++dec;                       /* ...increment for zero */

        len = j;

        j = 0;
```

```
        while (buff[len--] != '.')      /* length to decimal    */
            new[j++] = buff[len];       /* j has length         */

        i = 1;
        while (len >= 0)                /* Now place commas      */
            if (i % 4 == 0) {
                new[j++] = ',';
                i = 1;
            } else {
                new[j++] = buff[len--];
                ++i;
            }
        new[j--] = '\0';                /* Once inl, j forget null */

        i = 0;
        if (bucks)                      /* If $ wanted           */
            buff[i++] = '$';
        while (new[j])                  /* Copy back into buff   */

            buff[i++] = new[j--];
        buff[i] = '\0';
}
```

In main(), the user enters the number and indicates whether a leading dollar sign is desired. You could have called comma() with buff and avoided converting the number to a floating-point number in main(), but programs that might use comma() are more likely to have the number in floating-point format than a string. Therefore, the program calls comma() with three arguments: the number, a place to put the string result, and a flag for the optional dollar sign.

Once in comma(), the program calls the library function ftoa() to convert num to a string. The third argument in ftoa() is the precision wanted (2 digits after the decimal place), and the fourth argument states that the number is to be in floating-point format, not exponential. When ftoa() is finished, buff contains the string representation of the number.

The while loop is used to locate the decimal point. When the decimal point is found, the value of j is assigned to dec for later use. When the while loop terminates, j holds the length of the string, and dec the length to the decimal point. However, because j starts counting from 0, dec must be incremented once to represent character position rather than array position (because arrays start with element 0).

The `while(buff[len--]` loop copies the floating-point string into a temporary work space named `new[]`. Note how the copy works. Because `j` starts at zero but `len` equals the length of the string, the `while` loop produces in `new[]` a string representation that is the reverse of `buff[]`. That is, if `buff[]` is "1234.56", `new[]` contains "65." when the loop ends. Because a postdecrement is used in the `while`, the decimal point is also copied to `new[]`.

The function copies the string backward so that when the program senses the decimal point in "65.", commas will be inserted as every fourth element in the string from that point on. This makes things a lot easier than working with an nonreversed string.

The next `while` loop copies the rest of the string from `buff[]` to `new[]`, adding commas where appropriate. The variable `i` keeps track of where the function is in the string with respect to the decimal point and the insertion of commas. Whenever `i` equals 4, the modulo operator indicates that it is time to insert a comma in `new[]`.

When the `while` terminates, `new[]` contains a reversed copy of `buff[]` with the necessary commas added (for example, "65.432,1"). What does the following statement do?

```
new[j--] = EOS;
```

This statement places a string terminator (null) in `new[]` so that it can be treated as a string. But why the `j--` for the subscript? Because of the postdecrement, the null is written at the end of the string, and then `j` is decremented. This means that `j` now contains a subscript, not the null character, for the last character in the string. Without the `j--`, the null would be the first thing copied back into `buff[]` by the final `while` loop, and `buff[]` would appear empty.

The `if (bucks)` statement tests to see whether a leading dollar sign should to be added to the string. If the dollar sign has been requested (`bucks = 1`), it is the first character placed in `buff[]`. Variable `i` is postincremented so that the function does not overwrite the dollar sign in the final `while` loop.

The final `while` loop simply copies the formatted string in `new[]` back into `buff[]`. Again, the copy is done "backward" so that `buff[]` ends up with the proper contents.

Even though the function is fairly long, it is quite fast. If you need greater speed, however, try writing the function with character pointers instead of arrays.

6.10. The real reason for asking this question is to see whether you are susceptible to a common C programming error. Because the calculations involve floating-point numbers, each function that returns a noninteger value must be declared in the calling function that uses the return value.

```
/* Program to calculate monthly payment on loan */

#include <stdio.h>

main()
{
        double amount, rate, months, prompt(), pay();

        amount = prompt("Enter amount of loan: $");
        rate = prompt("Enter annual interest rate (15 = .15): ");
        months = prompt("Enter number of months for loan: ");

        printf("\nMonthly payment = %12.2f\n",
            pay(amount, rate, months));
}


/*****

        Function displays a prompt that is passed to it,
        accepts a line of input, and converts it to a floating-
        point number by a call to atof().

        Argument list: char *s        place to store the chars

        Return value: double        the converted input

*****/

double prompt(s)
char *s;
{
        char buff[30];
        char *gets();
        double atof();

        printf(s);                /* Show the prompt */
        return (atof(gets(buff)));
}
```

```
/*****

     Function that determines the monthly payment on a loan for
     the arguments supplied. Note that the interest rate is an
     annual amount, but the equation assumes a monthly rate.

     Argument list:  double a        amount of loan
                     double r        annual interest rate as
                                     a whole number (15=.15).
                     double m        number of months for
                                     loan

     Return value:   double          the monthly payment

*****/

#define MON_PER_YR  12.0

double pay(a, r, m)
double a, r, m;
{

     double power();

     r = (r * .01) / MON_PER_YR;

     return (a * r / (1.0 - 1.0 / power(1.0 + r, m)));
}
```

The program is fairly simple, but it has the potential trap of not declaring all variables that return a noninteger value. Notice that both prompt() and pay() are declared in main(). Failure to declare them causes the program to treat their return values in the context of an int data type, which may or may not lead to recognizable garbage.

The prompt() function takes the string constant (which resolves to a character pointer), prints the constant, and converts the user's input into a double data type. (Creating this function is easier than repeating the sequence of statements needed without the function.) Because atof() does the actual conversion, atof() must be declared to return a double in prompt().

The pay() function implements the equation for calculating the monthly loan payment. (One word of caution: Some compilers may reverse the arguments used in power(). Check your documentation.) Again, note that power() is declared to return a double.

Also note that floating-point 1 should be written as 1.0 so that the compiler recognizes the number as a floating-point constant, not an integer constant.

As a good learning exercise, try to dress up the program by adding direct cursor addressing, error checking on the inputs, printing the amount of interest paid, etc.

6.11. How many times did you have to read the quotation in the question before you started to design the algorithm? Often, programmers must read or listen to other people's "impressions" of what a program is to do. The ability to translate a verbal statement of a problem into an algorithm is a skill that increases with practice.

The key to the solution is to keep in mind that you must use numbers in both squared and cubed form. Therefore, it is unlikely that neither an int nor a long will work with reasonable data values. Further, because integer values are implied, the long data type seems to be the only logical choice.

```c
/* Program to test verbal algorithm presented in 6.11 */

#include <stdio.h>

main()
{
        char buff[20];
        char *gets();
        long i;
        long atol(), sumsq(), cubsum();

        printf("Enter ending integer: ");
        i = atol(gets(buff));

        printf("\nSeries up to %ld squared = %ld", i, sumsq(i));
        printf("\nand the sum of the
            integer cubed is %ld\n", cubsum(i));
}


/*****

        Function that sums the integers from i to 1 and returns
        the square of this sum

        Argument list: long i        ending value of series
```

```
      Return value:  long          square of sums

*****/

long sumsq(i)
long i;
{
       long sum = 0;

       while (i)
              sum += i--;

       return (sum * sum);
}

/*****

       Function that cubes the integers from i to 1 and returns
       the sum of the cubes.

       Argument list: long i        ending value of series

       Return value:  long          sum of the cubes of
                                     the series

*****/

long cubsum(i)
long i;
{
       long sum = 0;

       while (i)
              sum = sum + (i * i * i--);

       return (sum);
}
```

Notice that both functions use the same general approach to finding the sum of the series. In both functions, a while loop using a test on i controls the loop, and a postdecrement on the last i term prevents an infinite loop.

Would the program function the same if you changed the while loops to use, for example, a postdecrement as part of the expression that controls the while?

```
while (i--)
        sum = sum + (i * i * i);
```

The program does not function as before because i is first tested by the while and then immediately decremented. If, for example, the ending value of the series is 3, the first pass through the loop would never process the value of 3 because i would have been decremented to 2 before anything was calculated.

The pre- and postdecrement operators are handy, but they can be a nasty source of errors, especially when you are working with pointers.

As presented, the statement handles only positive numbers. This program could use the unsigned long int data type. Try rewriting the program, using unsigned long and verifying the results. The program should work.

6.12. A typedef is a shorthand notation for a previously declared attribute list (type definition). For example, suppose that you need several variables as flags in a program. These could be declared as

```
typedef int FLAGS;

FLAGS f1, f2, f3;
```

The beginner is sometimes confused about typedefs. A typedef cannot create a *new* data type. typedef only provides a convenient way to *summarize* the attribute list of a variable. In this example, the given attribute list for the typedef is that FLAGS is an int data type. Note that the attribute list for the typedef is added to the attribute list of the variable being declared. This concept can be summarized as

complete attribute list = variable's attributes + typedef

Consider a slightly more complex typedef:

```
typedef int ARRAY[];

ARRAY *flags;
```

In this case, the attribute list for the typedef is that ARRAY is an "array of ints." The attribute list for flags is pointer to ARRAY. Expanding ARRAY, we could say that the complete attribute list for flags becomes "pointer to an array of ints."

The key to deciphering a typedef's attribute list can be summarized in the mnemonic *calvat* (*complete attribute list = variable's attributes + typedef*). More is said about typedefs in the next chapter.

6.13. The student, for the offered example, is correct. However, the example is limited and misses the fullness of the typedef. A counter example usually makes the point.

```
typedef char BUFFER50[50];

BUFFER50 address, city;
```

The attribute list for BUFFER50 is "array of 50 chars." Therefore, address and city now have the same attribute list. The expanded declaration for the two typedefed variables is

```
char address[50], city[50];
```

A little thought should convince you that a #define cannot perform the same function in this example.

6.14. First study the sample program.

```
/* Examples of initializers for integers and characters */

#include <stdio.h>

char *emess = "help!\n";
char  prompt[] = "Enter the number:";

int vector[] = {1, 2, 3, 4, 5, 0};

int matrix[][3] = {
                {1, 2, 3},      /* row one   */
                {1, 4, 6},      /* row two   */
                {1, 8, 27}      /* row three */
        };

main()
{
        int i, j;

        printf(emess);
        printf(prompt);

        i = 0;
        while (vector[i])
                printf("%d ", vector[i++]);
```

```
for (i = 0; i < 3; ++i) {
        printf("\n");
        for (j = 0; j < 3; ++j)
                printf("%d ", matrix[i][j]);
}
}
```

The first thing to notice in this example is that character pointers and character arrays are initialized the same way because the compiler always resolves arrays to pointers. In most situations, the method used makes little difference. Recall from the discussion on pointers, however, that arrays are slightly slower than pointers but make it easier to "skip around" within the array. Pointers are usually best when the processing is sequential.

The program also initializes two integer arrays, the second of which is a two-dimensioned array. Notice how the last initializer in both cases does *not* have a comma after it. That is, the 0 in vector[] is not followed by a comma, but the other elements are. The braces are used to group the numbers in the vector[] array.

The two-dimensioned array named matrix[] must have the column value given (3, in this case). This is necessary so that the compiler knows where to "fold" the memory vector holding the array. Without the column value, the compiler would not know what scalar to use. Again, notice that braces are used to denote the grouping of aggregates and that the last aggregate does not have a comma following it.

Once the initialization has taken place, the program prints the contents of the arrays to demonstrate that all is as it should be. (If you did a sizeof(matrix), what would the answer be?)

Storage class does affect how aggregate data types, such as arrays, are initialized. Because all the variables initialized in the example are outside any function [including main()], they are of the external storage class and may be initialized using the initializer lists shown.

On the other hand, auto arrays cannot be initialized by the same method unless they have the static storage class. The only way to initialize auto arrays is by assignment.

7
Structures and Unions

Questions about Structures and Unions

7.1. What is a structure, and what is its general form? *(Answer on p. 172.)*

7.2. How is a member of a structure referred to? *(Answer on p. 173.)*

7.3. Using the people structure from 7.2, show the code necessary to initialize the first element of the structure array to contain the data associated with your own (member) data and that of a friend. *(Answer on p. 174.)*

7.4. How do you pass a member of a structure to a function? *(Answer on p. 174.)*

7.5. What is the proper syntax for passing a structure to a function? *(Answer on p. 175.)*

7.6. What two things should you be able to do with a structure on all compilers? What changes have been implemented on some compilers with respect to structures? *(Answer on p. 176.)*

7.7. Write a simple program that keeps the phone numbers of various friends. Use a structure for the desired information. (Although file I/O would be nice to use, you may not know anything about that subject yet, so don't use it.) *(Answer on p. 177.)*

7.8. What is the size of the following structure, and for what is it likely to be used? *(Answer on p. 180.)*

```
struct data {
     struct data *next;
     char name[30];
     unsigned income;
} demog;
```

7.9. What is a union? What syntax is used with it? *(Answer on p. 181.)*

7.10. Enter and run the following program.

```
          /* Potential surprises with unions and printf() */

#include <stdio.h>

union {
        int i;
        long big;
        double bigger;
```

```
} mixed;

main()
{
        mixed.bigger = 123.0;

        printf("bigger = %f", mixed.bigger);
        printf("\nbig = %ld", mixed.big);
        printf("\ni = %d", mixed.i);

        mixed.big = 1231;      /* Note: 123 el */

        printf("\n\ni = %ld", mixed.i);
        printf("\nbig = %ld", mixed.big);
        printf("\nbigger = %ld\n", mixed.bigger);
}
```

What, if anything, does the output suggest to you? *(Answer on p. 182.)*

7.11. What is the sizeof operator, and what is the advantage of using it in C programs? *(Answer on p. 183.)*

7.12. Write a program that breaks an int down into its individual bytes and shows what each byte holds in hexadecimal. Write this program so that it can be used on computer systems using either 2- or 4-byte integers. *(Answer on p. 184.)*

7.13. The Honeywell 6000 uses nine bits for a character, yet the program in 7.12 worked on this computer. Why did the program work? *(Answer on p. 191.)*

7.14. What does the statement

```
x = y == 5;
```

assign to x and why? *(Answer on p. 192.)*

Answers to Questions about Structures and Unions

7.1. A structure provides a way of organizing different data types so that they can be referred to as a single unit. I like the way Kim Brand describes structures: "arrays for adults." Arrays provide a means of referring to a group of identical data types (for example, an array of `int`s). Structures are more flexible; their contents can be any data type we've discussed. The general form of a structure is

```
struct tag {
     member1;
     member2;
            .
     memberN;
};
```

where `tag` is an optional *structure tag*. In the preceding form, no variable has been created by the structure declaration; only the mold for the structure has been created. The members (member1—memberN) can be any data types in any combination.

To create a structure from the mold, you must state the variable name to be associated with the structure. If you want a variable named `fluff`, the definition is

```
struct tag fluff;
```

The declaration instructs the program to take the structure mold named `tag` and create a variable called `fluff` from the mold.

The alternative way to define a structure is

```
struct {
     member1;
     member2;
            .
     memberN;
} fluff;
```

This method omits the optional structure tag and immediately defines the variable `fluff`.

If your program does not require two or more variables from the same structure mold, there's little reason to use a structure tag. A structure tag is designed to ease declaring multiple variables from the same structure.

The members of the structure can be whatever you want them to be. A simple structure might be

```
struct birthdate {
    int month;
    int day;
    int year;
};


struct birthdate mine, yours, theirs;
```

In this example, there are three variables (mine, yours, and theirs) molded from the same structure. Each structure contains three members, which are all integer data types (month, day, and year). Each data item defined within the structure is called a *member* of that structure.

To summarize, a structure is a collection of data items called members; unlike arrays, the members can be different data types. Structures provide a convenient means of organizing different data items and types so that they can be referred to as a single unit.

7.2. Referring to a member of a structure is easy if you remember the information the compiler needs to find the data associated with a member. The compiler must "know" which structure to use and to which member of that structure to refer. The operator used to accomplish this is called the "dot" operator (.). For example, if the structure is defined as

```
struct {
    char name[30];
    int sex;
    int age;
} people[100];
```

you have an array of 100 structures, each of which keeps one person's name, sex, and age. To print the name and age of the first person in the structure array, use

```
printf("The name is %s\n", people[0].name);
printf("and the age is %d", people[0].age);
```

The two pieces of information needed by the compiler are in the order you would expect: the structure name first, followed by the member wanted, with the "dot" operator separating the two pieces of information.

The general form for referring to a member is

structure_name.member_name

7.3. Suppose that your name is Jane Doe and your friend is John Smith, that 1 represents a female and 0 a male, and that you are 35 years old and John is 70. The code would be

```
struct {                          /* same as before */
     char name[30];
     int sex;
     int age;
} people[100] = {                 /* brace 1 ({)   */
          {"Jane Doe", 1, 35},    /* braces 2-3    */
          {"John Smith", 0, 70}   /* braces 4-5    */
};                                /* brace 6       */
```

Note the location of the braces after the equal sign. One set (braces 1 and 6) encloses all the initializers. Within these braces are matched pairs of braces surrounding each element of the array to be initialized (braces 2 and 3, and 4 and 5). Because only two elements of the `people` structure array have been initialized, the remaining 98 elements will be filled with zeros.

Finally, note that each array initializer *except the last one* is followed by a comma. If the list were for all 100 elements, it would be

```
} people[] = {                /* brace 1    */
     {"Jane Doe", 1, 35},     /* braces 2-3 */
     {"John Smith", 0, 70},   /* braces 4-5 */
                 .
                 .
     {"Emma Alkire", 1, 36}   /* NO COMMA   */
};                            /*            */
```

If Emma is the last person in the structure, no comma follows her initializer list.

To initialize the date structure from 7.1 with New Year's Day for 1985, use

```
struct birthday newyear = {1, 1, 1985};
```

Again, notice that no comma follows the last member of the structure. A fairly common mistake is to put a comma after the last structure member, but the compiler will get cranky if you do.

7.4. If the structure is declared as

```
struct {
     int a;
     int b;
} mine;
```

and you want to pass b to a function named process(), the function call is

```
process(mine.b);
```

What is actually sent to process() is a *copy* of whatever is in b when the function is called. If you want to change the value of member b in process(), you can use pointers (see next question) or you can use

```
mine.b = process(mine.b);
```

assuming that process() returns the new value of b from the function call.

7.5. First, to illustrate the proper syntax, suppose that a structure is

```
struct person {
      char name[30];
      int sex;
      int age;
} people;
```

The problem is that not all C compilers permit you to pass a structure to a function. However, for all C compilers that handle structures, you can pass the *address* of the structure to the function. Therefore, to give the function access to the structure, the syntax is

```
func1(&people);
```

This statement sends the address of people to the function, but func1() needs the contents of what has been passed to it. How does the function specify the argument list? Regardless of what func1() does, the function definition must be

```
int func1(friend)
struct person *friend;
{
      .
      /* We're assuming the function returns an int */
      .
}
```

The argument declarations inform func1() that it has been passed a pointer to the structure. If func1() is to determine whether an individual is over 21, the code might be

```
int func1(friend)
struct person *friend;

{
     int over21;

     over21 = (*friend).age / 21;

     return ((over21) ? 1 : 0);

}
```

The method of accessing a member is illustrated by

```
(*friend).age
```

The parentheses around person are necessary because the "dot" operator has precedence over the "indirection" operator (*). Verbalized, the statement translates: Go to the address of the person structure and get the member named age.

Because passing structures to a function is common in C, a shorthand notation (called the "arrow" operator) has been created:

structure_pointer->member_name

This notation

```
(*friend).age;
```

is the syntactic equivalent of

```
friend->age;
```

The "dot" operator is used to refer directly to a member of a structure. The "arrow" operator is used when a structure pointer is used.

7.6. Earlier questions in this chapter have shown that all compilers should be able to take the address of a structure and refer to a member of the structure. Some compilers also pass the entire structure to the function.

If your compiler supports passing structures (using the person structure from previous examples), the syntax is

```
int func2(stur)
struct person stur;
{
    int over21;
    . . .
    over21 = people.age / 21;
    . . .
}
```

The difference is that you no longer have to use a pointer to the structure. The "arrow" operator is not needed if the entire structure can be passed.

On UNIX System V, the C compiler supports passing structures to a function. The ANSI standards committee, which is working on the standards for the C language, will most likely recommend this trait also. The transition period will be messy, however, because some compilers will support the trait, whereas others will not, thus creating portability problems.

How you should write your code will, therefore, be fuzzy until the ANSI standard for C is adopted and published. Clearly, all compilers that support structures will support the "arrow" operator for pointer to structure. This avenue is more portable, but at the cost of economy of expression. Furthermore, this method may be either more or less efficient than passing the entire structure. How efficient the method is depends in part on whether you are writing for yourself or others and what compiler you are using. The question is difficult, and I don't think there is yet a "correct" answer.

If you are writing code for now that may be used on a variety of compilers, stick with the passing of the address of the structure. Any compiler that handles structures will handle the passing of a structure pointer.

7.7. Because the question removes the possibility of using disk data files to store the names, you must make the information part of the program itself. Given that constraint, what is the best approach? First, even though you expect the list to be stable, changes are likely. What is the best approach to the problem of maintaining the list?

If you code the names and numbers as string constants in the program, you will have to edit, recompile, assemble, and link the entire program whenever a change is made. On the other hand, if you keep the string constants in a separate file, you need to alter only that smaller file and relink it with the program file. On a small program like the following example, the amount of time saved is insignificant but can be considerable for larger programs.

File 1

Program File

```
                    /* Simple phone number program */

#include <stdio.h>

#define DEEP 21              /* Pause after DEEP lines */

struct phones {
        int area;            /* Area code */
        char num[9];         /* Number   */
        char name[30];       /* Name     */
};

main()
{
        extern struct phones friend[];
        char c;
        int i, lines;
        void pause();

        i = lines = 0;
        while (friend[i].area) {
                if (lines % DEEP == 0)
                        pause(&lines);

                printf("\n(%d)   ", friend[i].area);
                printf(" %s", friend[i].num);
                printf("      %s", friend[i].name);
                ++lines;
                ++i;
        }
}

/*****

    Function to pause display if more than DEEP lines are in
    program

    Argument list: int *line      pointer to line counter

    Return value: none

*****/
```

```
void pause(line)
int *line;
{
        if (*line) {
                printf("\n\nPress any key to continue: ");
                getchar();
        }

        printf("Area Code    Number    Name");
        printf("\n----------------------------");
        *line = 0;
}
```

The program first defines the structure for holding the phone numbers. The members are an int (area code) and two character arrays for the number and name. I chose to use a structure tag (phones) even though I could write the program without one.

In the main() function, the declaration

```
extern struct phones friend[];
```

indicates that you want to use an array of phones structures, but the array is defined somewhere else. The actual contents of the friend[] array is found in file 2.

File 2
Phone Numbers

```
struct {
        int area;
        char num[9];
        char name[30];
} friend[20] = {
        {317, "842-7162", "Fred"},
        {317, "123-4567", "Jim"},
        {317, "463-2000", "Sam"},
        {312, "321-7654", "John"},
        {317, "321-3213", "Jenny"}
};
```

The content of the structure is simple. Notice how the structure is initialized. Tell the compiler that you want 20 elements in the friend[] array, with each element containing the member's area, num[], and name[]. Then fill in information about 5 people as initializers for the friend[] array. Because the remaining 15 empty elements are not specified, they are filled in with zeros for the missing elements. This is why the test in the `while` statement

```
while (friend[i].area)
```

works as it should. The value of `friend[5].area` is 0, which the `while` loop treats as logical False, so the program ends. You can also use a `for` loop; any `while` can be expressed as a `for`. Either form allows you to add names and numbers to the `friend[]` array without modifying the source code of the program itself.

The `pause()` function delays the display when the screen is full. The statements for printing the header for the names and numbers are in `pause()`, so these functions do not need to be duplicated in `main()`. The first time through, `lines` equals 0, so `pause()` is immediately called before anything is on the screen. The function checks for this, so the program does not print the messages and wait for a key to be pressed. Although `lines` is 0 on the first pass, the function prints the header, clears the screen, and resets `lines`. (Because the program uses a pointer to `lines`, the value is changed by indirection.)

I will return to this example after I have discussed disk data files. It will increase the usefulness of the program substantially.

7.8. You can use the `sizeof` operator to determine the size of the structure

```
size = sizeof(demog);
```

If the size of both a pointer and an `unsigned` integer is 2 bytes, there are 34 bytes in the structure. Note that you do *not* have a structure within a structure. Rather, you have a *pointer to* another structure of the same type. The structure looks like the following diagram. (In the illustration `demog` is stored at memory location 50,000.)

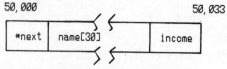

Typically, you would fill the structure with values. For the first person, `next` would be set to zero (null). After the first person is added, the diagram might look like

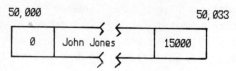

Now assume that you want to add another person to the list and that a call to `calloc()`

```
new = (struct data *) calloc(1, sizeof(struct data));
```

returns a pointer to enough storage for one structure of size data, the address of which is 51,000. After you fill in the structure so that it is diagrammed as follows,

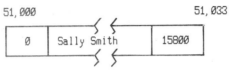

you want John Jones' record to be linked with Sally Smith's. You do this with the statements

```
struct data *ptr;
ptr = &demog;

ptr->next = new;
```

A diagram of the first structure now looks like

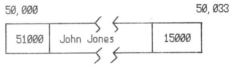

Therefore, this structure is often associated with a linked list. Whenever a new entry is made, the program assigns the address of the new structure to the next member of the previous structure. These pointers can be examined quickly to find the end of the list. [The end of the list always has a zero pointer value because `calloc()` initializes the storage to zero before a pointer is returned. This is another benefit to using `calloc()`.] The linked-list concept can also be applied to memory and disk storage.

Did you notice the cast we used on the call to `calloc()`? Remember that `calloc()` returns a "pointer to char." Since we wish a "pointer to struct data," we use the cast

```
(struct data *)
```

to shape the char * pointer from `calloc()` to the correct pointer for a structure of type data. Verify the form of this cast with the Right-Left rule.

7.9. A union is an amount of storage that can hold different sized items but only one piece of information at a time. For example, you might define a union as

```
union {
    int flag;
    long offset;
    double number;
} mixed;
```

The union named mixed is large enough to hold an int, a long, or a double, but only one data type can reside in the union at one time. To determine the storage requirements, the compiler uses the size of the largest data type that will reside in the union. Therefore, if a double requires eight bytes of storage,

```
i = sizeof(mixed);
```

produces a value of eight for i.

Suppose that you want to store a value in flag,

```
mixed.flag = i;
```

The syntax is identical to that of a structure, including the use of pointers.

Remember that the programmer must know what is in the union. If an int is in the union but you think it is a double, you may or may not get recognizable garbage. The C language itself provides no checks.

One purpose of a union is to serve as a temporary storage place for different types of variables. The temporary storage may be used for intermediate results of long calculations or for temporary values returned from function calls. Although not used often in typical C programs, unions are quite handy when they are needed. A union can save declaring a number of temporary variables.

The second and most common use of union is to examine types of data in different ways. We'll explore this method in question 7.12.

7.10. The purpose of this question is to let you see what your compiler does with data in a union when the printf() statements don't line up with what you think is in the union. (The actual result will vary greatly according to the compiler used.)

When I ran the program, the following results were printed:

```
bigger = 123.000000
big = 63111;
i = -2425

i = 19529851
big = 123
bigger = 123
```

Notice that the last two numbers produced the same result even though one was a double, and the other a long. The %ld conversion characters were used in both of the last two calls to printf(). This type of mistake can happen with a union. Because I thought a long was in mixed, I used a %ld conversion in printf(), but a double is actually in the union. The output looks perfect. Now suppose that you try to use bigger for a random-access call into a file. Will the double produce the correct results with disk file I/O?

This kind of mischief can make debugging more than a simple exercise, especially when printf()s are a central part of the debugging process. When you use a printf(), the conversion characters "assume" that you know the data type to be printed. As this example shows, even when you think that you have it right, the printf() "proves" that you do not have it right, because the data is not what you think it is.

7.11. The sizeof operator returns a number equal to the units of storage (bytes) required to store the item in memory.

The primary advantage of the sizeof operator is that it gives you a machine-independent method for allocating storage to a data item. A common use occurs when you do a call to calloc() that requires you to supply the number of items wanted and the size required for each. If, for example, you want enough storage for 100 ints, you might be tempted to use

```
ptr = calloc(100, 2);
```

because you know that an int takes two units of storage on most systems. The critical mistake lies in the phrase *on most systems*. This "good looking" code, if recompiled and run on another computer system, will "mysteriously" fail. The reason is that some C compilers allocate four bytes for an int. In other words, the use of calloc() as presented is not portable.

On the other hand, if you use

```
ptr = calloc(100, sizeof(int));
```

you will always get the correct storage for 100 ints regardless of the machine on which the program is compiled. Indeed, some programmers carry this practice one step further and use

```
ptr = calloc(MAX_ARRAY, sizeof(int));
```

This statement removes all constants from the call to `calloc()`. However, MAX_ARRAY must be #defined somewhere earlier in the program.

You should write every program with the idea that it might be taken to another environment. The liberal use of #define and sizeof will ease the job of porting your programs to other machines.

7.12. Again, this can be done a number of ways; the following is just one solution.

```
#include <stdio.h>

main()
{

        int intsize;
        int value;

        struct fourchars {
                char c1;
                char c2;
                char c3;
                char c4;
        };

        union examine {
                int i;
                struct fourchars bytes;
        };

        union examine intbytes;

        intsize = sizeof(int);
        value = 12345;
        intbytes.i = value;

        if (intsize == 2) {
                printf("%d in bytes is %x %x\n",
                        value, intbytes.bytes.c1,
                        intbytes.bytes.c2);
```

```
    } else if (intsize == 4)          {
            printf("%d in bytes is %x %x %x %x\n", value,
                intbytes.bytes.c1, intbytes.bytes.c2,
                intbytes.bytes.c3, intbytes.bytes.c4);
    } else {
            printf("Cannot analyze it!\n");
    }
}
```

The principal features of this program are the sizeof operator, which determines the size of an int, and a union that holds either an int or a structure.

We start by defining two ints: intsize, which will hold that size of an int; and value, which will hold the integer number that will be examined.

struct fourchars is declared to be a structure that holds four characters, c1 through c4. This is a structure declaration, not a structure definition. We have given a *tag* to this structure (fourchars) but have not told the compiler to allocate any space to hold this structure. Until we define a variable using struct fourchars, the compiler simply remembers the composition of the structure (that is, the "mold") but does not create any space in memory to hold the structure.

Next, the union examine is declared as

```
union examine {
        int i;
        struct fourchars bytes;
};
```

union examine can hold either an int or struct fourchars. Notice that we have given a variable name bytes to the structure. Later in this answer, we'll explain the reason for the name.

How big is union exmaine? The union will be large enough to hold its largest member. This means that union examine will never be less than four bytes long. We know that a char is large enough to hold a character and that char is defined as a byte. Therefore, we know that struct fourchars is four bytes long.

How long is an int? In the definition for this problem, we know that an int will be either two bytes or four bytes. From this definition, we know that the int will never exceed the size of struct fourchars, which is at least four bytes. This is why struct fourchars is declared to hold four characters and will be either larger than or the same size as int i.

The next line defines `intbytes` to be of type `union examine`, and the compiler allocates enough space to hold the union in memory.

The line

```
intsize = sizeof(int);
```

assigns to `intsize` the number of bytes needed to hold an integer. `intsize` will be used later to determine how many bytes should be printed.

The next line assigns a value to `value`—in this case, 12345. Any integer number can be used. In turn, `intbytes.i` is assigned from `value`, making `intbytes.i` equal to 12,345.

The notation in the assignment

```
intbytes.i = value;
```

assigns contents of `value` to the member `int i` in the union `intbytes`. The form for accessing a union member is the same as that for accessing a structure member. The notation for addressing a structure or union member is

struct/union_name.member_name

or

struct/union_pointer->member_name

if a pointer to a structure or union is used instead of the defined structure or union name.

The `if-else` test swings on the value of `intsize`. If `intsize` is two, the test is logical True, and the first `printf()` statement is executed. If the test is logical False, the `else` portion is executed. Note that this `else` portion controls another `if` statement, which tests whether `intsize` is equal to four. If this is logical True, the second `printf()` statement is executed. If `intsize` is neither two nor four, both `printf()` statements are skipped. This provision is for the possibility that the program is run on a machine whose `ints` are unconventional in size.

Note also that the two `printf()` statements cause the integer `value` to be printed, followed by the words "in bytes is." At this point, the two `printf()`'s vary. The first `printf()` prints the two characters in hexadecimal format (`%x %x`). The second `printf()` prints four characters in hexadecimal format (`%x %x %x %x`).

How do we access the character members of the structure? Earlier in this answer, we showed the form for accessing a member in a structure or union. What do we do when the member is another structure or union? We simply extend this form for another level of structure-member access.

To get c1 from the structure in the union, we used the following expression in the printf() statements:

    intbytes.bytes.c1

The form of this expression is

union_name.structure_name.member_name

The expression intbytes.bytes.c1 means, "Go to the union named intbytes. Inside it is a member called bytes. Inside bytes is a member called c1. Give the value of c1." Each dot simply steps one level deeper into the nested union or structure.

Notice the syntax of this expression. It uses the variable name of the structure or union, *not* the structure tag. To access the members of a nested structure (or nested union), the structure or union must have a defined name. If you do not name struct fourchars within the union, you will not be able to access the members of struct fourchars. In fact, struct fourchars will not even exist. To be a "real structure" (with allocated storage for the structure), it must be defined with a variable name.

In the program, the first printf() statement prints c1 and c2. The second printf() statement prints c1, c2, c3, and c4. Each prints the respective character, using the form just shown.

To see how we access the members, suppose that union intbytes is stored at memory location 50,000. The diagram shows the layout of the union for a 2-byte integer.

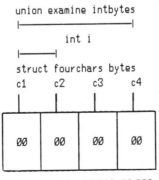

For a 4-byte integer, the union in memory appears as

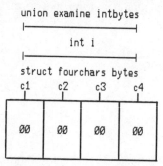

```
union examine intbytes
|———————————————————|
        int i
|———————————————————|
struct fourchars bytes
  c1      c2      c3      c4
```

50,000 50,001 50,002 50,003

Notice that the members in the union overlap. The *lvalue* of intbytes.i and intbytes.bytes. c1 is 50,000. The reason is that C guarantees that the first member of a structure or union will be placed at the front of the structure or union. No padding will ever appear there. This means that the c1 in struct fourchars bytes will be placed at the front of the structure. The "at-the-front rule" also means that the int i in intbytes also will be placed at the front of the union.

But how do we know that int i and struct fourchars bytes will have the same starting point in the union? C also guarantees that each member of a union will always start at the same memory location. Therefore, the *lvalue*s of int i and struct fourchars bytes must be identical.

Before the assignment, the *rvalue* of all members is 0. The reason is that C guarantees that when a structure or union is defined, all members are set to zero. Therefore, int i and struct fourchars bytes will be zero.

When the program executes the line

```
    intbytes.i = value;
```

a new *rvalue* (12,345) is given to int i, and the union in memory looks like

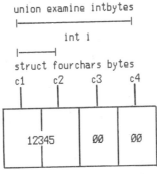

or

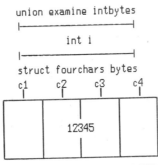

When we print the first byte of intbytes, we use the expression

    intbytes.bytes.c1

Because the *lvalue* of this expression is 50,000 and identical to the *lvalue* of intbytes.i, the *rvalue* will be the first byte in the integer i. The expression

    intbytes.bytes.c2

has an *lvalue* of 50,001, the next highest byte. The *rvalue* will be the next byte of the integer. This is true for c3 and c4. Each occupies the next highest byte in memory.

This program was tested on a variety of computers and compilers. The output from the program was

1. 12345 is 39 30
2. 12345 is 39 30 00 00
3. 12345 is 00 00 30 39

The ouput came from C compilers running on

1. Zilog Z80-, Intel 8086-, 8088-, and 80286-based computers

2. Intel 8088- and 80286-based computers; Digital Equipment VAX 11/780 and Honeywell 6000 computers

3. A Motorola 68000-based computer

The first output example was produced by compilers that used 2-byte ints. Each compiler produced the same answer. After the program was run, the results were verified by hand. 3930 hexadecimal is 14,640 decimal. Is this an error, or is there or flaw in the program?

No, there is no error or flaw. These machines reverse the order of the bytes that make up an int. 3039 hexadecimal is 12,345 decimal. From this program, we now know that the computer stores the least significant byte of an int first and the most significant byte last. Most computers work this way—reversing the order of the bytes.

The second result was produced on compilers that used 4-byte ints. By using a compiler that has 4-byte ints, the same computers using the Intel 8086 CPU family (8088 and 80286) produced four hexadecimal numbers, not two. The 4-byte ints were produced under compilers that used the "large memory model" for the Intel 8086 family. (Refer to Chapter 2 for more information.)

The VAX and Honeywell 6000 also produced the same results. The "native" int for these machines is four bytes large. Notice that these machines also store their numbers "backward," from least significant bytes to most significant bytes.

The last example was produced by a Motorola 68000 and shows that this CPU, unlike the others, is "backward" from other CPUs inasmuch as the 68000 stores numbers from the most significant bytes to the least significant.

This example highlights a very common application of a union: using a union to split apart and examine a different data type. We put an int into the union and retrieve the int as characters.

This facility is very powerful and prompts one major caveat. Storing one type of data into a union and extracting the data from the union as another type is machine-dependent, which means that this procedure may work on some computers but not on others. This approach must be used with caution.

Nevertheless, this approach is commonly used. For example, the Intel 8086 family can view some of its CPU registers as one 16-bit register or as two 8-bit registers. The AX register is a 16-bit register; AH and AL are half-registers that are 8 bits large. To access either, a union can be declared

```
union {
      int ax;
      struct {
            char al;
            char ah;
      } areg;
};
```

and the AX register can be addressed as an int or as two char-sized objects (al and ah). This type of approach (although the specific member names and data types within the union change) is used in handling the registers of almost all CPUs.

For an exercise, you might change this program to work with different data types, such as long int or double. Remember that the union and structure composition must be changed, and the if and printf() statements will also need to be changed. You can also change the program to accept a number from the keyboard rather than embed the number as a constant. This program can help you understand how your computer and compiler represent and store numeric information.

7.13 The reason why the program in 7.12 worked is that an int is four bytes long on the Honeywell 6000.

For an answer, the tip-off is that the Honeywell 6000 uses nine bits for a character. This means that a char is nine bits long.

Notice that we did a bit of defensive programming when we tested intsize for being either two or four. intsize gets its value from the sizeof(int) expression. If the 6000's int was a different size, the program would have printed

```
Cannot analyze it!
```

The sizeof(int) for this program is four. sizeof always returns the number of bytes of the tested object. Therefore, an int is four bytes long. Inasmuch as the C compiler for the Honeywell 6000 handles the sizes of char and int and we provided for a 4-char int, the program worked.

Because the program worked and a char is nine bits large, we can assume that a byte on the Honeywell 6000 is nine bits large, not eight. We can also deduce that an int on this machine is 36 bits large, not 32 bits (4 bytes times 9 bits per byte is 36 bits).

7.14. One advantage of C is its economy of expression: you can do a lot of work with relatively little code. This same economy of expression causes detractors of C to say that C is hard to read and understand. The terse example presented in this question may be a bit difficult to understand at first.

The only way to decipher what is assigned to x is first to determine which expression is executed first. Appendix A shows that the logical test for equality (==) has higher precedence than assignment (=). Therefore, the program first tests to see whether y equals 5. That is, the program first evaluates a logical test on y.

```
y == 5;
```

The value produced by a logical test can be only logical True (1) or logical False (0). The final value of x, therefore, will be 0 (if y is not equal to 5) or 1 (if y does equal 5). The evaluation of the statement can be diagrammed as follows:

Logical False	*Logical True*
x = y == 5;	x = y == 5;
x = 0;	x = 1;

It should be clear that order of precedence is not just an academic exercise. You need to learn the hierarchy of C operators. Not knowing the hierarchy (but assuming that you do) is a fertile source of program bugs.

8

Disk File Operations

Questions about Disk File Operations

8.1. We have included the contents of your compiler's standard I/O header file, typically called stdio. h, in many of the programs in this book. List the contents of stdio. h. What information is given in your version of stdio. h? *(Answer on p. 198.)*

8.2. What is the difference between high-level and low-level disk I/O? Which is better and why? *(Answer on p. 200.)*

8.3. The following program contains an error. Do not run the program until the error is corrected. What is the error, and what will happen if it is not fixed? *(Answer on p. 200.)*

```c
/* Simple program to copy a file */
/* CAUTION: PROGRAM CONTAINS ONE ERROR AS WRITTEN */

#include <stdio.h>              /* Include standard I/O header */

#define READ      *"r"          /* For reading a file       */
#define WRITE      "w"          /* For writing a file       */


void bell(), filerr(), filecopy();


main(argc, argv)
int argc;                       /* Command line argument count */
char *argv[];                   /* Pointers to them         */
{
        FILE *fpin, *fpout, *fopen();

        if (argc != 3)
           filerr("Usage: this_program file_to_be_copied
              copy_file_name"," ");

        if ((fpin = fopen(argv[1], READ)) == NULL)
                filerr("Cannot open %s\n", argv[1]);

        if ((fpout = fopen(argv[2], WRITE)) == NULL)
                filerr("Cannot open %s\n", argv[2]);

        filecopy(fpin, fpout);          /* Do the copy */

        printf("\nCopy completed\n");
}
```

```
/*****

        Function copies the contents of an input file into a
        new output file until end-of-file (EOF) on input

        Argument list: FILE *in       file pointer to input file
                       FILE *out      file pointer to output file


        Return value: none

*****/

void filecopy(in, out)
FILE *in, *out;
{
        char c;

        while ((c = getc(in)) != EOF)
                putc(c, out);

        fclose(in);
        fclose(out);
}

/*****

        Function to print a prompt string and one argument

        Argument list: char *prompt     pointer to the prompt
                       char *name        pointer to arg for prompt

        Return value: none

*****/

void filerr(prompt, name)
char *prompt, *name;
{
        bell();                         /* Assume you have this */
        printf(prompt, name);
        exit(1);
}
```

8.4. Rewrite the file copy program presented in 8.3 so that it uses low-level file I/O. (Hint: check your documentation for a header file called fcntl. h) *(Answer on p. 202.)*

8.5. As you know, `printf()` is an extremely versatile function. It is also necessarily complex and requires a considerable amount of code. Suppose that you want to print a short message and an integer number. What is the least "code intensive" way of doing it? *(Answer on p. 205.)*

8.6. Question 8.5 used the `fileno()` function to determine the file descriptor associated with `stdout`. Some compilers may not supply this function; but, as the previous question suggests, `fileno()` can be a handy function. Write your own version of `fileno()`. *(Answer on p. 207.)*

8.7. Some programs must be capable of sending output to both the CRT and the printer, depending on where the user wants the output sent. Write a short program that shows how you would solve the problem. *(Answer on p. 209.)*

8.8. One of my former students was hired to write a phone-in order system for a distributor. Part of the program required printing a description of an item on the screen. The problem was that some descriptions were short and others were very long. Fixed-record-length random-access files would have wasted considerable disk space for the shorter descriptions. (The company hoped that the remaining disk space would be needed for orders.)

To make things more concrete, work with the following assumptions. The descriptions vary from as few as 50 characters to as many as 600 characters for each product, and there are 500 products. Each product has a short product name (30 characters maximum). There is not sufficient storage to hold all the descriptions in memory. Without getting bogged down in too much detail, what would be your approach to the problem of quick retrieval of the descriptions without wasting disk space? *(Answer on p. 211.)*

8.9. You probably have developed your own C coding style by this time; and if you are like most people, you use many tabs. The use of tabs helps to make statements like `if`, `for`, `while`, and others easier to read. The problem, however, is that when you list the programs on the printer (egad! for debugging!), tabs sometimes cause lines to "fold," thus making the code more difficult to read.

C programmers often use filters to change some form of input to a different form on output. One useful filter changes to four spaces the tab character (`'\t'`) in a C program source file. In most cases, this alteration prevents long source lines and keeps deeply nested loops from folding.

Modify the copy program in 8.3 so that it filters a tab character into four spaces. When you've finished the program, test it on a C source file to see whether this modification preserves the intent of a tab but prevents folding on long or deeply nested lines. *(Answer on p. 214.)*

8.10. As you write longer programs, it becomes easier to forget which files define which functions. Usually, you can narrow the choice to two or three files, but that still means loading those files into a text editor until you find the desired function.

Write a program that accepts an input file name and a function name (or other variable, keyword, etc.) and lists all occurrences of that word in the file. Precede each source line with the proper line number and display the entire source line with the word on the display. *(Answer on p. 217.)*

8.11. Thus far, most of the examples have been concerned with writing ASCII characters to a data file. Obviously, you also need to be able to read and write numbers (in binary) to disk. Write a program that writes 50 binary numbers to disk and then reads them back. *(Answer on p. 222.)*

Answers to Questions about Disk File Operations

8.1. The following is a list of one stdio. h.

```
/****************** some system definitions ******************/

            #define NULL    Ø
            #define EOF     (-1)
            #define BUFSIZ  512


/****************** the iob structure ********************/

            struct  iobbuf{
                    int     _cnt;
                    char    *_ptr;
                    char    *_base;
                    int     _flag;
                    int     _fd;
                    };

    #define     _NFILE  6       /* maximum number of files */

    extern      int     _nfile; /* this variable yields the
                                    number of files set in
                                    the library */


    typedef     struct  iobbuf  FILE;

            extern  FILE    _iob[];

/********************* the iob definitions ******************/

            #define stdin    &_iob[Ø]
            #define stdout   &_iob[1]
            #define stderr   &_iob[2]
```

The standard I/O header file (stdio. h) usually has a number of #defines that are needed when disk files are used. Some of these are machine-specific (for example, a special character for EOF).

The file also defines the input-output buffer (iob) structure associated with the system I/O. The following is a typical example of the structure:

```
struct      iobbuf{
            int     _cnt;    /* Counter for characters */
            char    *_ptr;   /* Location of next char  */
            char    *_base;  /* Start of char buffer   */
            int     _flag;   /* How file is opened      */
            int     _fd;     /* File descriptor         */
            };
```

The iob structure forms the I/O heart of the system. The iob can be diagrammed as follows:

```
┌─────────────┐
│             │
│    _cnt     │
│             │
├─────────────┤
│             │
│   *_ptr     │
│             │
├─────────────┤
│             │
│   *_base    │
│             │
├─────────────┤
│             │
│   _flag     │
│             │
├─────────────┤
│             │
│    _fd      │
│             │
└─────────────┘
```

If pointers have a sizeof 2, each item in the iob has the same storage requirements. You cannot be sure where the two pointers point at this time. When you begin to use an iob, both pointers are initialized to point to a memory location that will be used for the character buffers. At the outset, both _ptr and _base point to the same memory location. As each character is moved into (or out of) the buffer, _ptr is incremented to point to the next character; but the _base pointer does not change. When the buffer is full, its contents are "flushed" (written) to the disk, _ptr is reset to equal _base, and the function is ready to begin again.

The _flag variable sets the mode in which you will use the iob (for example, read, write, or append). The _cnt keeps track of the number of characters that have been moved into (or out of) the buffer. The _fd is the file descriptor (fd) the programmer uses to refer to the file after it has been opened.

Notice that several of the iobs in stdio. h are already dedicated for specific uses.

```
/********************** the iob definitions ******************/
            #define stdin   &_iob[0]
            #define stdout  &_iob[1]
            #define stderr  &_iob[2]
```

The #defines are for standard input (stdin, keyboard), standard output (stdout, normally the video display), and standard error output (stderr, normally the same video display). Some compilers include a nonportable, but helpful, #define for the printer, usually called stdlst or stdprn. These definitions make it easy to redirect output from one I/O device to another.

You should compare your stdio.h file with these examples and keep a listing of your file handy for subsequent questions.

8.2. The major difference between high-level (HL) and low-level (LL) disk I/O is the way the operating system hands the data to the program. If you choose HL file I/O, you are free to manipulate the data any way you see fit. You can access as much data as you need—one byte at a time if you wish. However, the data is moved between the disk and your program, with LL file I/O, in chunks that are convenient for the host operating system.

Note that LL file I/O directly uses the file descriptor (see 8.1), but HL file I/O uses a pointer to the iob. The sequence of communications to file I/O in a program can be viewed in the following manner:

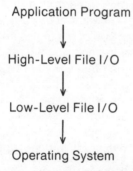

Application Program

↓

High-Level File I/O

↓

Low-Level File I/O

↓

Operating System

C gives the programmer the options of HL or LL file I/O for communicating with the operating system. If you choose HL file I/O, you actually move through the LL file I/O on your way to the operating system. LL file I/O gives a more direct link to the operating system.

This does not mean that LL file I/O is better. Different program requirements make one level better than the other in certain circumstances. Clearly, the safest route at this point is to learn both so that you can make informed decisions.

8.3. Because you have been warned not to run the program before correcting the error, you need to "walk through" the program first. The program begins properly with a #include of the standard I/O header file that contains the necessary information for using file I/O. Two #defines substitute READ for "r" and WRITE for "w" to open the two files for reading and writing. These substitutions make the fopen() call easier to read.

The program then checks to see whether three command-line arguments were used to invoke the program. These arguments are the program name, the file to be copied, and the new file to receive the copy. If these arguments are not supplied, the program calls filerr(), which prints a message that tells the user how the program should be invoked. The exit(1) call then terminates the program and returns the user to the operating system.

So far, everything looks fine.

The program then tries to open the input file and assign its FILE pointer to fpin. If the file cannot be found (or some other error occurs), filerr() is called with an error message, and the program terminates. The same logic applies to opening the output file and assigning its FILE pointer to fpout. If the file cannot be opened (for example, because the disk is full), the function calls filerr() to issue an error message and terminate the program.

Now that everything is set up, the program begins the actual copying of the file; the task is done by filecopy(). The two FILE pointers are passed to filecopy(). The function calls getc() with the FILE pointer for the input file (in) to read a single character from the input file. That character is assigned to c. The program checks c against EOF to see whether end-of-file has been read. If c is not an EOF character, the program calls putc() to write the character to the output file (using out). The program then closes both files by calls to fclose() with the appropriate FILE pointers. After returning from the filecopy(), the function prints a message stating that the file has been copied and ends the program.

On the surface, everything looks good. Where is the error? Look at filecopy() closely. Somewhere in stdio.h is a #define for EOF. Inspection shows that EOF is equal to -1. Can a char have a negative value with your compiler? Many compilers do not do sign expansion on the char data type, so the high bit is stripped and can never have a negative value. In this situation, a char can never sense EOF for the input file. As a result, the

```
while ((c = getc(in)) != EOF)
```

statement never terminates properly. The program will probably continue to copy something (Who knows what it might be!) until the disk is full.

The solution is to declare c in filecopy() to be an int so that the program can correctly sense EOF (a negative value). After this change is made, the program performs as it should.

8.4. The program remains much the same as before.

```c
/* Simple program to copy a file--low-level file I/O */

#include <stdio.h>              /* Include standard I/O header */
#include <fcntl.h>

#define MAXBUF  1024            /* Big input buffer         */

#define MODE    0               /* Right mode for my creat() */

#ifndef ERROR
        #define ERROR  -1       /* Need if not in stdio.h   */
#endif

void filecopy(), filerr();

main(argc, argv)
int argc;
char *argv[];

{
        int filein, fileout;

        if (argc != 3)
            filerr("Usage: this_program file_to_be_copied copy_file_name"," ");

        if (( filein = open(argv[1], O_RDONLY)) == ERROR)
                filerr("Cannot open %s\n", argv[1]);

        if (( fileout = creat(argv[2], MODE)) == ERROR)
                filerr("Cannot open %s\n", argv[2]);

        filecopy(filein, fileout, argv);

        printf("\nCopy completed\n");
}
```

```
void filecopy(in, out, argv)
char *argv[];
int in, out;
{
        char buffer[MAXBUF];
        int numbytes;
        while ((numbytes = read(in, buffer, MAXBUF)) > 0)
                if (write(out, buffer, numbytes) != numbytes)
                        filerr("error writing %s", argv[2]);

        close(in);
        close(out);
}


void filerr(prompt, name)
char *prompt, *name;
{
        bell();
        printf(prompt, name);
        exit(1);
}
```

As with all file I/O programs, you must #include the header file stdio.h. There are also some #defined constants in a file called fcntl.h. The most frequently used constants are

O_RDONLY	only read from this file
O_WRONLY	only write to this file
O_RDWR	read and/or write with this file
O_APPEND	start at the end of the file

With low-level I/O, reading, writing, or appending to a file correspond to the symbolic constants O_RDONLY, O_WRONLY, and O_APPEND, respectively, rather than to the respective quoted "r", "w", and "a" for high-level file I/O. The O_RDONLY and O_WRONLY symbolic constants simply make the code easier to read. By including fcntl.h in your program, you can use the proper compiler-specific constants needed for these functions.

Some additional #defines make the program easier to read and remove several constants from the code.

```
#define MAXBUF  1024        /* Big input buffer      */

#define MODE       0        /* Right mode for my creat() */
```

```
#ifndef ERROR
        #define ERROR      -1     /* Need if not in stdio.h */
#endif
```

Because low-level file I/O reads large chunks of data more or less directly from the operating system, you need some place to store the data read from disk. (Recall that the previous copy was done one character at a time.) Therefore, you #define MAXBUF to be 1024, although other values (for example, 128, 256, and 512) can be used.

The #ifndef preprocessor directive has the general form

```
#ifndef symbolic_constant
    .
    .
    .
#endif
```

If the *symbolic_constant* has not been defined at this point in the program, everything between the #ifndef and the #endif is compiled into the program. If the *symbolic_constant* has been previously defined (perhaps in stdio.h), the lines between the #ifndef and #endif are ignored. This practice provides a way to avoid duplicate definition errors.

Not knowing what is in the #include files is not necessarily ignorance. Different compilers may use different symbolic constants for the same thing. On many compilers, for example, EOF and ERROR have the same value but not the same meaning. The approach taken here gives the program a better chance of compiling on the first try.

The next thing to notice is that low-level file I/O uses file descriptors, not FILE pointers. The file descriptors are of the int data type. They do not use the FILE typedef. The program then checks the argument count. If that is correct, the function tries to open the input file with a call to open(). If the file cannot be opened, the program calls the filerr() function, which issues an error message and terminates the program.

Notice that the opening of the output file is different. A call to creat() is used to create the new file and return a file descriptor for use with the new file. (The error logic remains the same as in the preceding program.) creat() takes two arguments: the name of the file [as does fopen()] and a integer mode. The specific number for mode varies from compiler to compiler. I have used #defined

MODE to insert the right mode for my compiler. You should check your compiler's documentation for the MODE you should use.

Now that everything is set up properly, you are ready to copy the file. Once in filecopy(), the program defines buffer, a working buffer for storing the data as it comes off the disk, and the integer numbytes. The read() function has three arguments: the file descriptor (in), a place to put the data (buffer), and the number of bytes to be read (MAXBUF). The read() function returns the number of bytes actually read. The returned value from read() is assigned to numbytes. As long as numbytes is non-negative, the function has not reached the end of the file.

The write() call has the same number of arguments with the same functional purpose, but this function moves the data from the buffer to the disk, numbytes at a time. Because write() returns the number of bytes actually written, the value returned by write() should always equal numbytes. If it doesn't, an error has occurred, and filerr() is called. The function then closes the files and ends the program.

Although there are no firm rules, low-level file I/O should be somewhat faster than high-level I/O. The time difference will probably go unnoticed on most compilers but might be significant in programs that use a great deal of file I/O. As an experiment, time both versions of the copy program on a large file to see whether there is any noticeable difference.

8.5. If a dozen people answered this question, they would probably give a dozen different answers. One solution follows.

```
/* Write short program to print message and integer */

#include <stdio.h>

char mess = " hellos";

main()
{
        char buf[20];
        int i, device;
        char *itoa();

        i = 25;
        device = fileno(stdout);
```

```
        itoa(buf, i);
        write(device, buf, strlen(buf));
        write(device, &mess, 7);
}
```

You will recall from an earlier question that stdio.h predefines a number of input/output buffers (iobs) for stdin, stdout, stderr, and sometimes stdlst. On most machines, the numbers associated with the predefined iobs are 0, 1, 2, and 3, respectively. With this information, you can use the write() function to send output to the standard output device, the CRT. Using write() this way should make a program much smaller than one in which printf() is used.

However, the index associated with the iobs may vary with the compiler used. The purpose of the fileno() function is to return the file descriptor associated with an iob. The line

```
    device = fileno(stdin);
```

assigns device the file descriptor associated with stdin's iob. The file descriptor device is then used with write() to send information to the screen.

To print a number, you must first convert it to an ASCII string for display on the CRT. The call to itoa() converts the integer to an ASCII string. Because you may not know how long the string is (even though you do in this example), you can use the strlen() function to tell write() how many characters to write out. The same approach could have been used with mess; but instead, a numeric constant (7) was used to demonstrate an alternative way of printing the string.

The following program is almost equivalent to the preceding program and will give you some idea of the difference between the two methods.

```
/* Same program using printf() instead of write() */

#include <stdio.h>

char mess = " hellos";
```

```
main()
{
        char buf[20];
        int i, device;

        i = 25;
        printf("%d", i);
        printf("%s\n", mess);
}
```

Although other compilers may differ from mine, I found that the first version of the program used just under 2,500 bytes, and the second version with printf() generated just over 8,600 bytes of code. Therefore, the first program gives a two-thirds savings in code space. Even when the integer version of printf() is used (my compiler has a version of printf() that omits the floating-point routines), the second version of the program generates about 6,400 bytes of code, so the first version still gives a noticeable savings in code space.

Obviously, if you are not worried about code size or if you must use printf() for some reason, write() will not save you anything after printf() has been called into the program. In other situations, though, use of write() or other "less robust" functions, such as puts() or putchar(), will save needed code space.

As discussed in Chapter 5, the first program used the function itoa() to convert an integer to an ASCII string. If your compiler does not have a comparable function, forget the approach of using write(). The only available method to convert an integer to an ASCII string is to use sprintf(), which is another form of printf(). Using sprintf() is like using printf(), but you will increase the size of the program, not reduce it.

Another alternative is to write your own itoa()—a desirable but difficult task.

8.6. Your answer to this question will depend on the contents of your own stdio. h header file. Somewhere in that file you should find something that looks like the following:

```
/******************* the iob structure *********************/

            struct  iobbuf{
                    int     _cnt;
                    char    *_ptr;
                    char    *_base;
                    int     _flag;
                    int     _fd;
                    };
```

The structure member you are interested in, the file descriptor _fd, may have a different variable name in your header file; but you should be able to determine which variable is associated with the file descriptor. The following program shows how to write your own fileno() function. Use the name of the variable in your header file.

```
                /* Program to tell the fileno() function */

#include "stdio.h"

main()
{

        printf(" stdin = %d", fileno(stdin));
        printf("\nstdout = %d", fileno(stdout));
      . printf("\nstderr = %d\n", fileno(stderr));
}

/*****

        Function to determine which iobs are associated with the
        various file descriptors

        Argument list: FILE *ioptr     pointer to the iob structure

        Return value:  int             file descriptor as an int

*****/

int fileno(ioptr)
FILE *ioptr;
{
        return (ioptr->_fd);
}
```

As you can see, there isn't much to the function at all. You simply call fileno() with the pointer to the iob for which you want the file descriptor and ask for the member of that iob which holds the file descriptor (_fd).

A call to fileno() returns an integer value of the file descriptor (fd) for the iob requested. This fd can then be used with the write() function.

8.7. The standard library has a function called fprintf(), which has the following general form:

```
void fprintf(fp, control, args)
FILE *fp;
char *control, args;
{

          .

}
```

We know that stdout is a FILE pointer and fprintf() will work with stdout. What about the printer?

If your compiler provides stdlst, which is also a FILE pointer, all you need is a way to direct the output through stdout or stdlst. If your compiler does not offer stdlst, you will need to fopen() the printer. The rest of the program is basically the same.

```
/* Program to toggle output between CRT and printer */

#include <stdio.h>

#define PRINTER "prn"            /* printer name for my compiler */

main()
{
     int age, i;
     FILE *fp;                   /* Pointer to iob structure     */
     FILE *fopen();

     age = 21;

     while (TRUE) {
          printf("Output to\n1. CRT  2. Printer");
          printf("\n\nEnter 1 or 2: ");

          i = getchar() - '0';    /* Make into an int */
          if (i > 0 && i < 3)     /* Within range ?   */
               break;
     }
```

```
    #ifdef stdlst

        fp = (i == 1) ? stdout : stdlst;

    #else

        if(i == 1)
            fp = stdout;
        else

        if ((fp = fopen(PRINTER, "w")) == NULL) {
            printf("\nCannot open the printer\n");
            exit(1);
        }

    #endif

        fprintf(fp, "\nHer age is %d\n", age);
    }
```

The program must #include the standard I/O header file (stdio.h) and then declare a few working variables, including fp as a typedefed FILE pointer and the function fopen().

Next, the program asks the user where to send the output. The while loop gets a character and converts it to an int by subtracting 'Ø' from the character digit entered. If a 1 or a 2 is entered, the program control breaks out of the while loop.

The #ifdef stdlst controls whether we will compile the code to use stdlst or the code to explicitly open and use the printer. If stdlst is a #defined name, the line containing the ternary will be compiled. Otherwise, the code to open the printer will be compiled.

The ternary assigns a FILE pointer to fp based on the value of i. If i is 1, fp is assigned the value of the pointer for stdout. Otherwise, fp is given the value to the pointer to stdlst (the printer).

The #else performs a similar function as the ternary. If i is 1, fp is assigned the value for stdout. If i is not 1, a call to fopen() is made using the #define name for the printer as the file name. If fopen() returns a NULL pointer, we could not open the printer for output. An error message is displayed, and we exit the program. If fopen() was successful, fp has a FILE pointer that can be used to send characters to the printer. The program uses fprintf() to display a short message on the selected output device and then ends.

You can use the same approach to direct the output to a disk data file. If you have a third option for disk file output (assuming that you have a proper file name and write mode), assign the fp during a different call to fopen(). The subsequent call to fprintf() then sends its output to the designated disk file.

The value of the #define name for PRINTER can vary among compilers and operating systems. You should check your compiler's documentation for the equivalent name for your printer, if your compiler does not use stdlst.

8.8. C does, of course, provide for random-access files. However, fixed record lengths waste too much disk space. (The vendor has a popular micro with a 10-megabyte hard disk.) You need a random-access method for variable-length fields within the file.

Assume that the first product is called DSDD 5.25 Disks and has a 75-character description. The second item, SSSD 8.0 Disks, has a 50-character description. You want your program to display the short (30-character) product names on the screen and let the user select one. After an item is selected, you want to print its full (variable-length) description. Therefore, you want the short product names read from disk into memory at the start of the program and the long descriptions retrieved from disk as they are requested by the user.

One approach is to create two data files: one for the short product names and one for the long descriptions. The first file might be viewed as follows:

```
struct {
    char sname[31];          /* Don't forget the null */
    long offset;
} small[500];
```

In the first file, an array of 500 structures is defined, each of which has two members: sname[] and offset. Why is offset a long data type? The reason is that the function lseek(), which you will use to index into the long description file, uses a long to position itself in a file.

When the small[] array is written to disk, the array might look like the following diagram (the data file is small.dat):

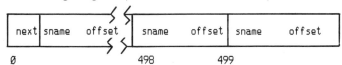

The variable next in the file is a long that points to the next empty record in the data file. Because you will be using byte pointers, the value of next before anything is entered in the file is sizeof(long)—4 on most systems.

You need a program that enters both the short product name (as held in small[]) and the longer description to be stored in the second data file.

The second data file might look like the following diagram (big.dat):

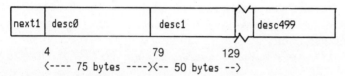

As in the smaller file, the variable next1 shows the location of the next empty record in the file and is initialized with sizeof(long) before any data is written to the file.

Now enter the first item. First, the program opens the two data files and reads next and next1. The variable next indicates where the short item name goes in small.dat. Variable next1 indicates where the long description for this item is found in big.dat. You can assume that the name of the first item (DSDD 5.25 Disks) has been entered directly in small[0].sname[]. You now need to fill in the proper byte offset in big.dat:

```
small[0].offset = next1;
```

When this is done, you can write small[0] to small.dat. (You can assume that the file is open and that fd1 is the file descriptor for small.dat.)

```
lseek(fd1, next, 0);       /* put us 4 bytes into file */
write(fd1, small[0], 35);  /* each element is 35 bytes */
```

The reason next, next1, and small[].offset are long data types is that lseek() *must* have a long as its second argument.

Now assume that the long description of the item has been placed in a character array called buff[]. The description is 75 characters long including the null, so you can use it as a string. To write the long description to big.dat, use the following:

```
lseek(fd2, next1, 0);         /* put us 4 bytes into file */
write(fd2, buff, strlen(buff) + 1);
```

You need to add 1 to the strlen() because the null is not included in calculating the length of the string, but you want to store the null in the file.

Now all you have to do is update the file offsets:

```
next += 35;          /* each small[] is 35 bytes */
next1 += strlen(buff) + 1;
```

and write the new values back to disk:

```
lseek(fd1, 0L, 0);    /* Puts us at file beginning */
write(fd1, next, sizeof(long));

lseek(fd2, 0L, 0);
write(fd2, next1, sizeof(long));
```

When you have completed these procedures, the two files will look like the following diagrams:

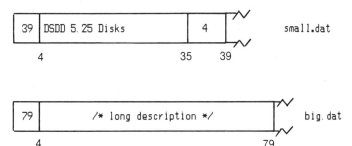

Notice that small[0]. offset has a value of 4, the correct offset into big. dat to get the long description for this item.

It should be clear that small[1] goes at byte position 39 in small. dat and that the long description for the next item starts at byte position 79 in big. dat. Prove to yourself that after the next item is added (a 50-character description including the null for the string), next will equal 74, and next1 will equal 129.

After the two files have been built, all you need to do is read from disk small. dat and display it. When the user picks an item from the list (for example, item x), small[x]. offset gives the exact offset position of the long description in big. dat. One lseek() and a read(), and you have the long description.

Other variations could be used, but this one is simple and fairly fast. To gain experience using low-level file I/O, try experimenting with this approach on a problem of your own.

8.9. Filters are very useful in a wide variety of situations, and this program is useful in its own right. In fact, the program listing of the filter has been "run through itself" to give you an idea of what the result looks like.

```
/* Simple program to copy a file--high level file I/O */

#include <stdio.h>          /* Include standard I/O header */

#define READ   "r"          /* For reading a file */
#define WRITE  "w"          /* For writing a file */
#define MAXBUF 1024         /* Big input buffer   */

#ifndef ERR
    #define ERR -1          /* Need if not in stdio.h */
#endif

main(argc, argv)
int argc;
char *argv[];
{
    FILE *filein, *fileout, *fopen();

    if (argc != 3)
        filerr("Usage: this_program file_to_be_copied copy_file_name"," ");

    if (( filein = fopen(argv[1], READ)) == NULL)
        filerr("Cannot open %s\n", argv[1]);

    if (( fileout = fopen(argv[2], WRITE)) == NULL)
        filerr("Cannot open %s\n", argv[2]);

    printf("\nStarting the filter...");
    filecopy(filein, fileout, argv);

    printf("\nfilter completed\n");
}

void filerr(prompt, name)
char *prompt, *name;
{
    bell();
    printf(prompt, name);
    exit(1);
}
```

```
/* Filter: change tabs to EXPAND blank spaces as part of copy */

#define TAB     '\t'      /* Tab character    */
#define EXPAND  4         /* Tab = 4 spaces   */
#define OLDTAB  8         /* Old tab value    */


/*****

    Function copies the contents of an input file into a new
    output file until end-of-file (EOF) on input. If a tab
    character (TAB) is found, it is replaced in the file with
    EXPAND blank spaces.

    Argument list: FILE *in      file pointer to input file
                   FILE *out     file pointer to output file

    Return value: none

*****/

void filecopy(in, out)
FILE *in, *out;
{
    int c, flag, i, pad;

    pad = 0;
    while ((c = getc(in)) != EOF) {
        if (c == TAB) {
            if (pad == 0 || (pad % EXPAND) == 0) {
                for (i = 0; i < EXPAND; ++i) {
                    putc(' ', out);
                    ++pad;
                }
                continue;
            }
            i = pad % EXPAND;
            if (i)
                for ( ; i < EXPAND; ++i) {
                    putc(' ', out);
                    ++pad;
                }
            if (pad % OLDTAB == 0)
                ;
            else
```

```
                    for (i = 0; i < EXPAND; ++i) {
                        putc(' ', out);
                        ++pad;
                    }
            } else {
                putc(c, out);
                if (c == '\n')
                    pad = 0;
                else
                    ++pad;
            }
        }

    fclose(in);
    fclose(out);
}
```

Since we are using file I/O, we first include `stdio.h` and declare several symbolic constants. The `#ifndef ERR` says that, if ERR is not already defined (in `stdio.h`), define ERR to be -1. Note that we must use command line arguments (`argv`) to get the input and output file names from the user. Two FILE pointers are then declared for the input and output files. It also declared that `fopen()` returns a FILE pointer.

The first thing the program does is check whether three command line arguments were given. (By the way, the error message associated with an incorrect number of command line arguments "wrapped around" before being processed by the filter.) The program then tries to open the input and output files. If they cannot be opened properly, an error message is printed, and the program ends. If all goes well, a message to that effect is displayed, and we call `filecopy()`.

Note the use of the `#defines` before `filecopy()`. My text editor uses eight spaces for a tab, and I decided to reduce it to four spaces. You should adjust yours accordingly. A more flexible approach would be to make these parameters (that is, 4 and 8) command line arguments. However, since I tend to use only one text editor, I chose this approach. (Extra credit if you use command line arguments!)

The logic in `filecopy()` is a little more complex than you might expect because we are trying to preserve the amount of indentation at all levels. For example, if a tab is eight spaces and you just typed a variable name with nine letters, simply inserting four spaces for the next tab will cause a loss of alignment.

When a tab is read from the input file, note what has to be done to maintain alignment. We use the modulo operator in the expression

```
pad % EXPAND
```

to find out whether we are on an even tab boundary or not. The variable pad keeps track of where we are in the line. If pad is zero, we must be at the beginning of a line. If we find a tab with pad equal to zero, or if pad % EXPAND is zero, we simply print out EXPAND blank spaces.

If pad was not zero, we have found a tab somewhere after the beginning of a line. We assign i to hold the number of spaces needed to maintain alignment by using the modulo operator again. If i is nonzero, the if (i) is logical True, and we output the desired number of blank spaces.

Next, we see whether the current character counter in pad is an even boundary relative to the old number of spaces in a tab (pad % OLDTAB). If this is true, we don't have to do anything. A situation like this would arise if pad were 24 and OLDTAB were 8. If pad % OLDTAB is nonzero, we output the new number of spaces (that is, EXPAND).

If something other than a tab is read from the input file, we simply copy the material to the output file. The process keeps repeating itself until EOF is read, at which time the program ends.

To convince yourself of what is actually going on, first try writing the program as one that simply replaces a tab with EXPAND spaces and look at the output. Then, having seen the results, reread the preceding narrative. Once you've seen what the output looks like without alignment correction, the discussion will take on new meaning.

8.10. Because this program differs in some ways from the earlier one, the entire program is presented here.

```c
/* Find each source line that matches a given word */

#include <stdio.h>

#define READ   "r"      /* For read                  */
#define MAXSTR  256     /* Max string length         */
#define STOP    22      /* Number of line before pause */
#define EXPAND "   "    /* Use 3 blanks for tabs     */


char buff[MAXSTR + 1];  /* place for it              */

void bell(), look(), filerr(), pause();
```

```
    main(argc, argv)
    int argc;
    char *argv[];
    {
            char search[MAXSTR];
            FILE *fpin, *fopen();

            if (argc < 3)
               filerr("Usage: this_program file_to_search string"," ");

            if ((fpin = fopen(argv[1], READ)) == NULL)
                 filerr("Cannot open %s\n", argv[1]);

            strcpy(search, argv[2]);

            look(fpin, search);

            printf("\n\nEntire file read");
    }

/*****

    Function searches each source line for a match on the word
    supplied on the command line. It prints the line number
    where a match was found, followed by the entire source line.

    Argument list: char pattern[]      word to match
                   FILE *in            fp for input file

    Return value: none

    CAUTION:  Several additional lines of code are necessary
              because the CP/M operating system translates all
              command-line arguments to uppercase. This
              function converts them back to lowercase but
              will lose distinction for uppercase symbolic
              constants (for example, #define TAB will look
              like tab on output).

*****/

void look(in, pattern)
char pattern[];
FILE *in;
{
```

```
int c, i, j, line, test, pstop;

pstop = line = 0;

while ((c = getc(in)) != EOF) {
        c = toupper(c);      /* CP/M causes uppercase */
                             /* Convert for match     */
        i = 0;
        if (c == '\n')
                ++line;
        else
                buff[i++] = c;

        while ((c = getc(in)) != EOF && c != '\n')
                buff[i++] = toupper(c);   /* CP/M toupper() */
        buff[i] = '\0';

        j = 0;
        while (j <= i) {
                if (buff[j] == pattern[0]) {
                        test = strncmp(&buff[j], pattern, strlen(pattern));
                        if (!test) {
                                ++pstop;
                                printf("\nLine %d ", line);
                                while (buff[test]) {
                                        if (buff[test] == '\t') {
                                                printf(EXPAND);
                                                test++;
                                        }
                                                /* CP/M tolower() */
                                        printf("%c", tolower(buff[test++]));
                                }
                                if (pstop % STOP == 0 && pstop != 0)
                                        pause(&pstop);
                        }
                }
                ++j;
        }

        if (c == '\n')
                ++line;
}                              /* End while ((c = getc()... */

fclose(in);
}
```

```
/*****

    Function to print a prompt string and one argument

    Argument list: char *prompt     pointer to the prompt
                   char *name       pointer to arg for prompt

    Return value: none

*****/

void filerr(prompt, name)
char *prompt, *name;
{
        bell();
        printf(prompt, name);
        exit(1);
}

/*****

    Function delays the screen and waits for user to press a
    key before the display continues. It resets the line counter
    to 0.

    Argument list: int *num     line counter in calling function

    Return value: none

*****/

void pause(num)
int *num;
{
        printf("\nPress any key to continue: ");
        getchar();
        *num = 0;
}
```

The program begins by checking for the correct argument count. After the source file to be used is opened, the program copies into the search[] array the word for which you want to search and calls look().

The look() does all the work. Some working variables are first declared, and pstop and line are set to zero. Both variables are line counters; line counts the lines in the source file, and pstop counts the number of lines displayed on the CRT. Variable pstop causes the display to pause when STOP lines of output have been displayed.

The while loop calls getc() to read a character from the source file and tests it against EOF. If c is not an EOF, the character is converted to an uppercase letter by the call to toupper(). The CP/M operating system converts all command-line arguments to uppercase, so you must convert the source to uppercase to find a match.

This may not be necessary with your operating system. If it passes the command line to your program as typed, you can eliminate the toupper() calls. Specifically, MS-DOS and UNIX programmers can eliminate the toupper() calls.

The function then checks for a newline and increments line if it finds one; otherwise, the program places the character in buff[]. The next while loop is used to copy one source line into buff[]. MAXSTR determines how long a source line can be. Again, the call to toupper() is necessary because of CP/M. If case translation is not done, these CP/M-specific calls can be eliminated.

When the program senses an EOF or a newline, the inner while loop terminates, and a null is moved into buff[]. Note that the string length of buff[] is given by i.

The program then looks through buff[] for a match on pattern. If the character in buff[] matches the first character in pattern[], the function calls strncmp() to see whether a complete match exists. The function strncmp() compares two strings, but only up to the first n characters. The call to strlen(pattern) tells strncmp() what the n value is.

Because strncmp() returns a 0 for a match, an if (! test) will be logical True only if there is a match. The function then increments the display-line counter (pstop), prints the line number, shrinks any tab expansions to EXPAND blank spaces, and prints the buffer a character at a time. (I could have done a simple string print, but I decided to convert back to lowercase for printing. The uppercase letters look too much like BASIC code.)

The program then tests pstop to see whether a call to pause() is needed to give the user time to read what is on the screen. If no call is necessary, the program increments j to continue looking through buff[]. The procedure repeats until an EOF is sensed.

There are several niceties you might add. For example, it would be nice to be able to direct the output to the screen, printer, or disk file. It wouldn't be too difficult to do a search for more than one word. (This is harder than it appears at first, however, because a space on the command line is taken to be another `argv[]`. The `argv[]`s must be concatenated to form a complete `pattern`.) These enhancements (and others) would increase the utility of the program, although it is very useful as is.

8.11. The program can be written using either high- or low-level file I/O. I chose to use high-level file I/O to illustrate the use of several functions not previously discussed.

```c
/* Writes and reads MAXNUM binary numbers to and from disk */

#include <stdio.h>

#define FILENAME "NUMBERS.DAT"   /* Name of data file */
#define MAXNUM        50          /* Number to write   */
#define WRITE        "w"
#define READ         "r"

void readint(), wrtint();

main()
{
        int array[MAXNUM], i;
        FILE *fp, *fopen();

        if ((fp = fopen(FILENAME, WRITE)) == NULL) {
                printf("\nCannot open %s for write", FILENAME);
                exit(1);
        }

        printf("\nWriting data...\n\n");
        wrtint(fp, MAXNUM);       /* Write 50 numbers */

        if ((fp = fopen(FILENAME, READ)) == NULL) {
                printf("\nCannot open %s for read", FILENAME);
                exit(1);
        }

        printf("Reading data...\n\n");
        readint(fp, array);       /* Read them   */

        for (i = 0; i < MAXNUM; ++i)
                printf("%d ", array[i]);
}
```

```
/*****

      Function writes num integers to disk

      Argument list: int num        maximum passes through loop
                     FILE *fp        file pointer for open file

      Return value: none

*****/

void wrtint(fp, num)
int num;
FILE *fp;
{
      int i;

      for (i = 0; i < num; ++i)
              putw(i, fp);              /* Write 2 bytes */

      fclose(fp);
}

/*****

      Function reads MAXNUM "wordsize" items from disk and stores
      them in val[].

      Argument list: int val[]       array for storing words from
                                      disk
                     FILE *fp         pointer to the open file

      Return value: none

*****/

void readint(fp, val)
int val[];
FILE *fp;
{
      int i;

      for (i = 0; i < MAXNUM; ++i)
              val[i] = getw(fp);       /* Read 2 bytes */

      fclose(fp);
}
```

The program should look quite familiar by now. The two functions highlighted are putw( ) and getw( ).

The putw( ) function has two arguments: the integer value to be written and the fp associated with the file. The function does not actually "know" that it is writing integers but simply that it has to write "wordsize" bytes to disk. Wordsize can vary among machines, but two bytes is typical.

The getw( ) function is the converse of putw( ) and uses just the fp for its argument. The function fetches wordsize bytes from the disk file associated with the argument fp passed to it. Again, getw( ) doesn't "know" what it's getting, just the number of bytes to read from the disk.

In your compiler's documentation, you should find similar functions for reading other multiples of wordsize bytes from disk. You might also find functions that get and put both the long and double data types. You might want to use the program in this question as a form but change the putw( ) and getw( ) to one of the other data types, such as putl( ) and getl( ).

9

Preprocessor Directives and Odds and Ends

Questions about Preprocessor Directives and Odds and Ends

9.1. How does a #define work? For what should a #define *not* be used? *(Answer on p. 227.)*

9.2. What is the #if preprocessor directive? Also explain the #else preprocessor directive. Give an example of how each might be used. *(Answer on p. 228.)*

9.3. What is the #ifdef preprocessor directive, and how does it work? *(Answer on p. 229.)*

9.4. What is a *parameterized macro* in C? Give an example of a parameterized macro that squares a number. *(Answer on p. 230.)*

9.5. Discuss the advantages and disadvantages of using #include files instead of the alternatives that C offers to accomplish the same task. *(Answer on p. 231.)*

9.6. Can #ifs be nested? *(Answer on p. 232.)*

9.7. What is the #undef preprocessor directive? How might it be used? *(Answer on p. 232.)*

9.8. What are #asm and #endasm preprocessor directives? *(Answer on p. 232.)*

9.9. What is the enum data type, and how is it used? *(Answer on p. 233.)*

Answers to Questions about Preprocessor Directives and Odds and Ends

9.1. The #define is a *text* replacement within the source code of the C program. For example,

```
#define MAXSTR 50
```

causes 50 to be placed in the source code wherever MAXSTR appears in the program. MAXSTR is not a variable, nor is the #define a C statement. If it were, it would have a semicolon at the end of the #define.

Consider what will happen if you place a semicolon at the end of a #define:

```
#define MAXSTR 50;
```

The following code will appear later in the program:

```
char array[MAXSTR];
```

After the preprocessor pass of the compiler, the char declaration will appear as

```
char array[50; ];
```

because the #define is a text replacement for whatever follows the symbolic constant being defined. Clearly, this is not going to pass the syntactic parser of the compiler. To make things worse, the source code appears correct. Fortunately, most compilers catch a semicolon at the end of a #define.

Knowing when not to use the #define is also important. I've seen code similar to the following:

```
#define INT 2        /* Number of bytes in an int */
```

The programmer was trying to call attention to a machine-specific code so that changing it would be easier if the program were taken to an environment where an int was not two bytes. The intention is laudable, but the approach can be improved. As you have seen earlier, the sizeof operator was created for the purpose of solving the problem this programmer was trying to address.

Although there will be situations where you must use machine-specific #defines, using them for operations that the sizeof operator can solve is inappropriate.

9.2. The general form of the #if is

```
#if symbolic_constant
    compile this
#endif
```

A common example of the #if arises in testing and debugging a section of code. Suppose that you are putting numbers in an array and that you need to print the array before you continue the program. Your source code might look as follows:

```
#define DEBUG 1          /* 1=on, 0=off */

#include <stdio.h>

main()
{
    ...
    #if DEBUG

        for (i = 0; i < VAL; ++i)
            printf("%d ", array[i]);

        getchar();

    #endif

    ...
}
```

While you are testing the code, DEBUG is turned on with a value of 1. Because the #if works much the same as a normal if, a nonzero value for DEBUG means that the lines between the #if and #endif will be compiled into the program.

When the program is debugged and tested and everything checks out, the #define can be changed to

```
#define DEBUG 0
```

When the program is recompiled, the code between the #if and #endif is not compiled into the program. This method gives you a way of leaving the test code in the source program but deleting it from the executable code.

The #if can also be used with a #else. For example,

```
#if ADDS
    char clear[] = "\014";
#else
    char clear[] = "\033*";
#endif
```

The function is the same as the `if-else` construct. Depending on the value of ADDS, the program will declare the clear-screen codes for an ADDS terminal or a TeleVideo. In fact, if you wish, you can also use the following form:

```
char clear[] =
#if ADDS
    "\014";
#else
    "\033*";
#endif
```

This form works the same way as the first version. Neither has preference because both result in the same code being compiled into the program.

9.3. The `#ifdef` is similar to the `#if` (discussed in 9.2). The `#ifdef` means that if the symbolic constant has been defined at this point in the program, the function will include in the program the source lines that follow the `#ifdef`. The `#endif` marks the end of the lines that are controlled by the `#ifdef`. For example,

```
#ifdef CPM
    int user_name;
#endif
```

causes `user_name` to be compiled into the program only if CPM has been previously defined with a nonzero value. This preprocessor directive allows you to toggle certain sections of code into and out of the program, depending on the existence of specific symbolic constants in the program. Note that, unlike the `#if`, the `#ifdef` depends on the symbolic constant's existence instead of its value.

You can also use the `#else` with the `#ifdef`:

```
#ifdef CPM
    int user_name = 1;
#else
    int path_name = 1;
#endif
```

The function compiles one of the two declarations into the program, depending on whether CPM has been previously defined.

The declared variable might be used later to decide which operating system (or whatever) is being used, and the function will take appropriate action based on the variable.

The preprocessor also recognizes the reverse of the #ifdef: the #ifndef, which means "if not defined." The CPM example could have been written as

```
#ifndef CPM
     int path_name = 1;
#else
     int user_name = 1;
#endif
```

This function produces the same results, but the logic is inverted.

9.4. A *parameterized macro* consists of a #define for a symbolic constant, followed by a statement of how the symbolic constant is expanded. To square a number, you might write

```
#define SQR(x)      (x) * (x)
```

There must not be any space between the symbolic constant and the opening parenthesis. SQR (x) won't work.

When the preprocessor finds

```
SQR(x)
```

in the source file, it treats the expansion as

```
(x) * (x)
```

As a result, you can find the square of a number by using a parametized macro instead of using a function call or coding the calculation directly.

Are the parentheses necessary around the x? They are not required, but it is safer to use them. Consider what will happen if the macro is

```
#define SQR(x)  x * x
```

and your program uses SQR as

```
if (TRUE)
     SQR(num - 2);
```

When you finish the expansion, it becomes

```
if (TRUE)
     num - 2 * num - 2;
```

What does the expression produce if num equals 5? What you want is 3 squared. However, because of the hierarchy of operators, the expression evaluates as though it were

```
num - (2 * num) - 2;
```

That is not what you expect. To be safe, enclose parametized macros in parentheses.

In stdio.h, you will sometimes find putchar() and getchar() defined as parametized macros. They might appear as

```
#define putchar(c)   putc(c, stdout)
#define getchar()    getc(stdin)
```

which shows that calls to putchar() and getchar() are actually calls to putc() and getc().

One advantage of parametized macros is that they are data-independent. Using the SQR(x) example, you can square any number with the parametized version. This would not be the case if a function call were used.

9.5. A #include reads a C source code file into the program containing the #include. The file is read into the program at the point of the #include; the file is not appended to the source file.

The advantage of a #include file is that it allows one file (usually called a header file) to contain all variables, preprocessor directives, and similar elements that are common to other source code programs. If changes are needed to anything in the header file, only one source file needs to be edited. After the necessary changes have been made, the programs using the header file can be recompiled. All programs then incorporate those changes. A #include file lends consistency because only one file is changed and recompilation ensures that every file is changed consistently.

If the designed purpose of a #include is followed, there really are no disadvantages. However, #includes can be misused in the sense that they contain code (for example, functions) that can be compiled separately and then linked into the program. For example, if a function definition in a #include file is used in several programs, you must recompile every program that uses the #include file. On the other hand, if the function stands alone in its own module, you need to recompile only that file and then relink the programs. If relocatable forms of the programs are available, this method saves time because linking is faster than recompiling and linking.

Usually, a `#include` file contains little more than preprocessor directives and global declarations. Rarely does this file include function or data definitions.

9.6. Yes. See, for example, the following:

```
char day[] =
#if   DAYS == 1
      "monday";
#else
#if   DAYS == 2
      "tuesday";
#else
#if   DAYS == 3
      "wednesday";
#endif
#endif
#endif
```

The only thing to notice is that you must have `#endif` for every `#if` you use. Obviously, the preceding code can work only with the external storage class because it is initializing a character array.

9.7. The general form is

```
#undef symbolic_name
```

The purpose of the `#undef` is to "undefine" some previously defined symbolic constant.

The `#undef` is normally used to affect subsequent preprocessor directives (such as a `#if`) and their impact on subsequent action in the program.

9.8. Technically, `#asm` and `#endasm` are not part of the standard for the C language. However, various compiler manufacturers have added these directives to the preprocessor pass. The purpose is to allow assembly language code to be compiled into the program.

The advantage is that a part of the program which, for whatever reasons, was too slow can be replaced by assembler to increase speed. The disadvantage is that the resultant source code is nonportable unless you rewrite the source program or provide a new assembler section.

If your compiler supports these preprocessor directives, they may prove useful at some time (assuming you know assembler). Keep in mind, however, that you are writing code that is less portable.

9.9. The enum data type is part of the UNIX System V's C compiler, but not part of the C standard yet. The general form for declaring an enum data type is

enum *identifier* {*val1, val2, ...valn*};

where

identifier is the name associated with the enumerated data type

and

valn indicates the permissible values the enumerated variables may take

For example,

```
enum person {male, female};
enum person sex;
```

means that sex is of type person and the only values which can be assigned to sex are male or female.

What values are associated with male and female? The compiler treats both as constants. The compiler starts with integer 0 and assigns that value to the first name (male = 0); the second name is assigned 1 (female = 1); and so on, until the list is finished.

You may want a value to be something other than the value assigned by the compiler's sequential integer assignment. The statement

```
enum person {male, female = 39};
```

overrides the default assignment value (that is, 1) for female and replaces it with 39.

Note that the statement

```
sex = male;
```

is valid, but

```
sex = 0;
```

is not valid. You can assign enumerated constants only to an enum variable.

You can also make the same enum data type by using

```
enum {male, female = 39} sex;
```

The variable sex has the same meaning as before.

A
Order of Precedence

Rank	Operator	Association
1	( ) *function call* [] -> .	left to right
2	! ^ ++ -- (cast) sizeof	
	* *indirection* & *address of* - *unary minus*	right to left
3	* *multiply* / %	left to right
4	+ -	left to right
5	<< >>	left to right
6	< <= > >=	left to right
7	== !=	left to right
8	& *binary AND*	left to right
9	^ *binary XOR*	left to right
10	| *binary OR*	left to right
11	&&	left to right
12	||	left to right
13	?:	right to left
14	= += -= *= /= %= <<= >>= &= ^= |=	right to left
15	,	left to right

B
Binary and
Assignment Operators

Binary Operators

Operator	Use
+	addition
-	subtraction
*	multiplication
/	division
%	modulo division
>>	right shift
<<	left shift
&	bitwise AND
		bitwise OR
^	bitwise exclusive OR (XOR)

Assignment operators

Operator	Example	Comment
=	x = 1;	Simple assignment
+=	x += 1;	Same as x = x + 1;
-=	x -= 1;	Same as x = x - 1;
*=	x *= 2;	Same as x = x * 2;
/=	x /= 2;	Same as x = x / 2;

```
%=         x %= 2;          Same as x = x % 2;
>>=        x >>= 3;         Same as x = x >> 3;
<<=        x <<= 3;         Same as x = x << 3;
&=         x &= 0x7f;       Same as x = x & 0x7f;
|=         x |= 0x7f;       Same as x = x | 0x7f;
^=         x ^= 0x7f;       Same as x = x ^ 0x7f;
```

C
ASCII Codes

The codes for the American Standard Code for Information Interchange, or ASCII, are listed below. These codes are given for those numbering systems commonly used in C. A control character is abbreviated as ^; a Control-C is shown as ^C.

Decimal	Hex	Octal	Binary	ASCII
0	00	000	00000000	null (NUL)
1	01	001	00000001	^A (SOH)
2	02	002	00000010	^B (STX)
3	03	003	00000011	^C (ETX)
4	04	004	00000100	^D EOT
5	05	005	00000101	^E ENQ
6	06	006	00000110	^F ACK
7	07	007	00000111	^G (bell) BEL
8	08	010	00001000	^H (backspace) BS
9	09	011	00001001	^I (tab) horizontal HT
10	0A	012	00001010	^J (linefeed) LF
11	0B	013	00001011	^K (vertical tabs) VT
12	0C	014	00001100	^L (formfeed) FF
13	0D	015	00001101	^M (carriage return) CR
14	0E	016	00001110	^N SO
15	0F	017	00001111	^O SI
16	10	020	00010000	^P DLE
17	11	021	00010001	^Q DC1
18	12	022	00010010	^R DC2
19	13	023	00010011	^S DC3
20	14	024	00010100	^T (DC4)
21	15	025	00010101	^U (NAK)
22	16	026	00010110	^V (SYN)

Decimal	Hex	Octal	Binary	ASCII
23	17	027	00010111	^W (ETB)
24	18	030	00011000	^X (CAN)
25	19	031	00011001	^Y (EM)
26	1A	032	00011010	^Z (SUB)
27	1B	033	00011011	Escape
28	1C	034	00011100	FS
29	1D	035	00011101	GS
30	1E	036	00011110	RS
31	1F	037	00011111	US
32	20	040	00100000	Space
33	21	041	00100001	!
34	22	042	00100010	ʺ
35	23	043	00100011	#
36	24	044	00100100	$
37	25	045	00100101	%
38	26	046	00100110	&
39	27	047	00100111	ʹ
40	28	050	00101000	(
41	29	051	00101001	)
42	2A	052	00101010	*
43	2B	053	00101011	+
44	2C	054	00101100	,
45	2D	055	00101101	-
46	2E	056	00101110	.
47	2F	057	00101111	/
48	30	060	00110000	0
49	31	061	00110001	1
50	32	062	00110010	2
51	33	063	00110011	3
52	34	064	00110100	4
53	35	065	00110101	5
54	36	066	00110110	6
55	37	067	00110111	7
56	38	070	00111000	8
57	39	071	00111001	9
58	3A	072	00111010	:
59	3B	073	00111011	;
60	3C	074	00111100	<
61	3D	075	00111101	=
62	3E	076	00111110	>

Decimal	Hex	Octal	Binary	ASCII
63	3F	077	00111111	?
64	40	100	01000000	@
65	41	101	01000001	A
66	42	102	01000010	B
67	43	103	01000011	C
68	44	104	01000100	D
69	45	105	01000101	E
70	46	106	01000110	F
71	47	107	01000111	G
72	48	110	01001000	H
73	49	111	01001001	I
74	4A	112	01001010	J
75	4B	113	01001011	K
76	4C	114	01001100	L
77	4D	115	01001101	M
78	4E	116	01001110	N
79	4F	117	01001111	O
80	50	120	01010000	P
81	51	121	01010001	Q
82	52	122	01010010	R
83	53	123	01010011	S
84	54	124	01010100	T
85	55	125	01010101	U
86	56	126	01010110	V
87	57	127	01010111	W
88	58	130	01011000	X
89	59	131	01011001	Y
90	5A	132	01011010	Z
91	5B	133	01011011	[
92	5C	134	01011100	\
93	5D	135	01011101	]
94	5E	136	01011110	^
95	5F	137	01011111	_
96	60	140	01100000	`
97	61	141	01100001	a
98	62	142	01100010	b
99	63	143	01100011	c
100	64	144	01100100	d
101	65	145	01100101	e

Decimal	Hex	Octal	Binary	ASCII
102	66	146	01100110	f
103	67	147	01100111	g
104	68	150	01101000	h
105	69	151	01101001	i
106	6A	152	01101010	j
107	6B	153	01101011	k
108	6C	154	01101100	l
109	6D	155	01101101	m
110	6E	156	01101110	n
111	6F	157	01101111	o
112	70	160	01110000	p
113	71	161	01110001	q
114	72	162	01110010	r
115	73	163	01110011	s
116	74	164	01110100	t
117	75	165	01110101	u
118	76	166	01110110	v
119	77	167	01110111	w
120	78	170	01111000	x
121	79	171	01111001	y
122	7A	172	01111010	z
123	7B	173	01111011	{
124	7C	174	01111100	|
125	7D	175	01111101	}
126	7E	176	01111110	~
127	7F	177	01111111	del, rubout

Index

More Computer Knowledge from Que

Que Order Line: **1-800-428-5331**

All prices subject to change without notice.

LEARN MORE ABOUT C WITH
THESE OUTSTANDING TITLES FROM QUE

Advanced C:
Techniques and Applications

by Gerald E. Sobelman and David E. Krekelberg

Concentrating on the C language's more complex features, *Advanced C* is for those who already have a working knowledge of the C language. Divided into three parts, this book explains C's advanced features; the implementation of complex data structures; and applications of the language, including graphics and techniques for constructing advanced user interfaces. If the reader is a C programmer, an applications designer, an engineer, or a student of computer science, *Advanced C* will increase one's knowledge of the C language.

C Programmer's Library

*by Jack Purdum, Ph.D., Tim Leslie,
and Alan Stegemoller*

Polish your C programming skills. This easy-to-follow book clears the confusion that often complicates learning C. Makes the C language comprehensive.

. . . an outstanding contribution to developing facility in C programming. . . . Invaluable work.

THE STOCK MARKET MAGAZINE

C Programming Guide, 2nd Edition

by Jack Purdum, Ph.D.

To accommodate current revisions of the C software program, Que is publishing a second edition of the *C Programming Guide*. This tutorial book expands and updates the reader's knowledge of the applications introduced in the first edition. The second edition of *C Programming Guide* gives readers numerous examples and illustrations to help them learn how to program in C. Users won't want to miss the second edition of one of the best-selling C programming tutorials on the market.

Common C Functions

by Kim Brand

This book displays dozens of C functions that are designed to teach C coding techniques and provide useful building blocks for program development. One chapter focuses on the elements and structures of C programming and explains how to read and understand C code written by others. If you want to gain a stronger understanding of C code and how it works, *Common C Functions* is a superb guide. All the C code in this book is also available on disk.

Mail to: Que Corporation • P. O. Box 50507 • Indianapolis, IN 46250

Item	Title	Price	Quantity	Extension
179	Advanced C: Techniques and Applications	$19.95		
148	Common C Functions	$17.95		
188	C Programming Guide, 2nd Edition	$19.95		
45	C Programmer's Library	$19.95		
		Book Subtotal		
	Shipping & Handling ($1.75 per item)			
	Indiana Residents Add 5% Sales Tax			
		GRAND TOTAL		

Method of Payment:

☐ Check   ☐ VISA   ☐ MasterCard   ☐ American Express

Card Number _____ Exp. Date _____

Cardholder Name _____

Ship to _____

Address _____

City _____ State _____ ZIP _____

If you can't wait, call **1-800-428-5331** and order TODAY.

All prices subject to change without notice.

FOLD HERE

- -

_____

_____

_____

_____

7999 Knue Road
Indianapolis, IN 46250

Save Time and Effort!

C Self-Study Guide Companion Disk

Only $39.95

A perfect companion for *C Self-Study Guide*, this handy disk will be available in January, 1986. The disk contains C programs that are explained and studied in the book. Use this convenient disk to:

- Speed up the learning process.
- Eliminate the time-consuming task of manual entry.
- Ensure the accuracy of each program line.
- Gain immediate access to useful C programs.

Order your convenient disk today. Use the form below to order the popular IBM PC format. Call Que at 1-800-428-5331 to ask about the availability of other formats.

Mail to: Que Corporation • P. O. Box 50507 • Indianapolis, IN 46250

Please send _____ copy(ies) of the *C Self-Study Guide* programs on an IBM PC format disk ($39.95 each).

Subtotal	$ _____
Shipping & Handling ($2.50 per item)	$ _____
Indiana Residents Add 5% Sales Tax	$ _____
TOTAL	$ _____

Method of Payment

☐ Check   ☐ VISA   ☐ MasterCard   ☐ AMEX

Card Number _____ Exp. Date _____

Cardholder's Name _____

Ship to _____

Address _____

City _____ State _____ ZIP _____

If you can't wait, call **1-800-428-5331** and order TODAY.

All prices subject to change without notice.

CSSG-8511

FOLD HERE

_____

_____

_____

_____

Que Publishing, Inc.
7999 Knue Road
Indianapolis, IN 46250

REGISTRATION CARD

Register your copy of *C Self-Study Guide*. Just complete this registration card and return it to Que Corporation. You will also receive the latest information about Que's newest products relating to the C programming language and the UNIX operating system.

Name _____

Address _____

City _____ State _____ ZIP _____

Phone _____

Where did you buy your copy of *C Self-Study Guide?*

_____

How do you plan to use the programs in this book?

_____

_____

What other kinds of publications about C and UNIX would you be interested in? _____

_____

Which C compiler do you use? _____

Version number _____

Which operating system do you use? _____

Which computer? _____

THANK YOU!

CSSG-8511

FOLD HERE

_____

_____

_____

_____

C Self-Study Guide Registration
Que Corporation
7999 Knue Road
Indianapolis, IN 46250

0215